TOPIK UNLOCK

SONALI GANGWAR

Contents

CONTENTS

Foreword

Welcome to "TOPIK Unlock: Your Ultimate Guide to Conquering the Korean Language Exam"! As you hold this book in your hands, you're embarking on a transformative journey into the vibrant world of Korean language proficiency.

In these pages, you'll find invaluable insights, practical tips, and proven strategies to help you navigate the complexities of the Test of Proficiency in Korean (TOPIK) Level exam. Written by Sonali Gangwar, a dedicated language enthusiast and TOPIK Level graduate, this book is your trusted companion on the path to success.

Whether you're a novice learner or seeking to enhance your existing skills, "TOPIK Unlock" is designed to meet you where you are and propel you toward your language learning goals. With Sonali's expertise and friendly guidance, you'll feel empowered to tackle each chapter with confidence and enthusiasm.

So, prepare to unlock new opportunities and broaden your horizons through the mastery of Korean language proficiency. Let's embark on this exciting journey together!

Happy studying!

Preface

Welcome to "TOPIK Unlock: Your Ultimate Guide to Conquering the Korean Language Exam"! I'm thrilled to share this comprehensive resource with you as you embark on your journey to mastering the Test of Proficiency in Korean (TOPIK) Level 1 exam.

As a passionate language enthusiast and proud TOPIK Level 2 graduate, I understand the challenges and excitement that come with learning a new language. In this book, I've poured my heart and soul into creating a roadmap that will guide you through the intricacies of the TOPIK exam, providing you with the tools and strategies you need to succeed.

Through personal anecdotes, expert advice, and practical exercises, "TOPIK Unlock" aims to demystify the exam process and empower you to achieve your language learning goals. Whether you're studying independently or with a tutor, this book is designed to support you every step of the way.

I hope you find this book helpful and inspiring as you embark on this enriching journey of language discovery.

Sonali Gangwar

Acknowledgments

Writing "TOPIK Unlock: Your Ultimate Guide to Conquering the Korean Language Exam" has been an incredible journey, and I am deeply grateful to everyone who has contributed to its creation and success.

First and foremost, I would like to express my heartfelt gratitude to my family for their unwavering support and encouragement throughout this endeavor. Their belief in me has been a constant source of strength.

I am also indebted to my friends and fellow language enthusiasts who have provided valuable insights, feedback, and encouragement along the way. Your enthusiasm for language learning has inspired me to push boundaries and strive for excellence.

I extend my sincere appreciation to the team at our publishing house for their professionalism, expertise, and dedication to bringing this project to fruition.

Last but not least, I am profoundly grateful to the readers who have chosen to embark on this journey with me. Your passion for learning and commitment to personal growth are truly inspiring.

Thank you all for being a part of this adventure.

Introduction

Hey there, and welcome to "Mastering TOPIK 1: Your Ultimate Guide to Success in 15 Days." This is where our adventure begins – a journey to conquer the Test of Proficiency in Korean (TOPIK) Level 1 exam in just 15 days. Whether you're starting from square one or refreshing yourKorean skills, this eBook is here to be your trusty companion every step of the way.

The TOPIK 1 exam is like a key that unlocks the door to show off your basic Korean language skills. Through this guide, we'll not only break down the exam's structure, format, and scoring butalso give you the confidence boost you need to tackle it head on.

Over the next two weeks, we're diving deep into tried-and-true strategies, effective study techniques, and tailor-made practice exercises. Think of it as your coach, guiding you through theups and downs of language learning.

So, are you ready to embark on this whirlwind journey to language mastery? Let's dive in togetherand kickstart your transformation into a bona fide Korean language whiz!

1. Understanding the Topik 1 Exam

Let's dig into what the TOPIK 1 exam is all about! Think of it as our map to mastering Korean injust 15 days.

Structure: Picture the TOPIK 1 exam like a two-sided coin: Listening and Reading. The Listening part tests how well you understand spoken Korean, while the Reading section checks if you get the gist of written Korean texts.

Format: Each part has its vibe. In the Listening bit, you'll tune in to audio clips and pick the right answers. Meanwhile, the Reading segment, it's all about tackling passages and nailing those comprehension questions.

Scoring: Now, about those scores – it's like a game of aiming for that sweet spot. You haveto hit at least 80 points in each section and rack up an overall score of 140 to ace the exam.

Preparation: Getting ready for the TOPIK 1 means getting cosy with how it works. Dive into the question types, practise your listening skills, and speed-read through Korean texts.

Knowing the ins and outs of the TOPIK 1 exam sets the stage for your prep journey. It's like understanding the rules before diving into a game. So, let's gear up and dive into the next chapter, where we'll plot out your study plan. Ready to roll? Let's do this!

2. Setting Goals and Schedules

Step	Actions
Define Your Goals	- Set specific objectives
	- Solve previous year's papers
	- Break goals into daily tasks
Create a Study Schedule	- Allocate time for each task
	- Morning: Vocabulary drills
	- Afternoon: Reading comprehension
	- Evening: Listening practice
Stay Flexible	- Adjust schedule as needed
	- Be forgiving of setbacks
Track Your Progress	- Keep a study journal
	- Note improvements and challenges

3. Essential Grammar and Vocabulary

15-Day Vocabulary Mastery Journey

In the vocabulary section of "Mastering TOPIK 1: Your Ultimate Guide to Success in 15 Days," you'll find a valuable PDF resource packed with essential words to boost your Korean language skills. By diligently mastering 120 words daily from this PDF and dedicating time to practise grammar over 15 days, you'll be well on your way to excelling in the TOPIK 1 exam. With consistent effort and focused practice, you'll expand your vocabulary and strengthen your understanding of grammar structures, setting a solid foundation for success in the exam. So, dive into the PDF, commit to learning new words daily, and prioritise grammar practice – your journey to TOPIK 1 proficiency awaits!

Essential Grammar

Vocabulary for Beginners

Essential Grammar

Type 1. 아/어/여~ 계

Type 2. -(으)~ 계

Type 3. 자음 시작~ 계

Type 4. 조사

Type 5. 접사

Type 6. 부정 부사

TYPE 1. 아/어/여~ 계

Pattern	Meaning/Usage
아/어/여 드리다	Offer to do something for someone else
아/어/여 보다	Conveys meanings like 'someone tries doing something' or 'someone does something to see how it will turn out'
아/어/여 주다	Expresses the speaker's request for something
아/어/여 보이다	Conveys meanings like likeness, resemblance, or similarity
아/어/여야겠다	Informal polite speech style
아/어/여도	Expresses 'even if, even though'
아/어/여도 되다	Asks for and gives permission
아/어/여서 1	Indicates cause or reason
아/어/여서 2	Used when the subject performs one action and then a second one
아/어/여야 되다/하다	Expresses obligation or necessity

TYPE 2. -(으)~ 계

Pattern	Meaning/Usage
-(으)ㄴ 지 (시간) 되다	Expresses an interval of time extending from the past to the present
-(으)ㄴ 적이 있다	Indicates one's past experiences
-(으)ㄴ/는/을 것 같다	Expresses the speaker's thought or opinion
-(으)ㄹ 거예요	Informal ending of the future tense; expresses a supposition or intention
-(으)니까	Indicates reason and cause
-(으)ㄹ 수 없다/있다	Indicates ability, capability, possibility, or permission
-(으)ㄹ 때	Indicates 'while'; used with all verbs and adjectives
-(으)ㄹ 줄 알았다	Used to express knowledge or lack of knowledge of a technique or process
-(으)ㄹ게요	Indicates the speaker's intention, plan, or promise
-(으)ㄹ래요	Used to inquire about someone's opinion or view

TYPE 3. 자음 시작~ 계

Pattern	Meaning/Usage
(명사)+ 때문에	Indicates 'because of', 'owing to', 'as a result of', 'in consequence of'
-거나	Means 'and', 'or', 'even though', 'no matter how', 'whatever'
-게 되다	Expresses that the situation has been arranged by certain environmental facts or conditions
-고 싶다	Indicates desire
-군요	Used to express surprise, delight, or wonder
-기 때문에	Indicates cause and reason

TYPE 4. 조사

Pattern	Meaning/Usage
이/가	Indicates that the preceding noun phrase is the subject of the sentence
에서,	Indicates 'at' or 'in', 'from'
-까지,	Expresses the finishing point of the action
-와/과,	Means 'and', 'with', 'along (together) with'
-한테,	Used for indicating the receiver of an action

TYPE 5. 접사

Pattern	Meaning/Usage
들	Plural form of the noun
-쯤,	Means 'around... o'clock'

TYPE 6. 부정 부사

Pattern	Meaning/Usage
못	This means impossibility or strong denial and refusal
안	Expresses the negative and means 'do not'

VOCABULARY FOR BEGINNERS

No.	한글	English	No.	한글	English
1	가게	store, shop	41	감사하다	thank, appreciate
2	가격	price	42	감사합니다	thank you

#	Korean	English	#	Korean	English
3	가구	furniture	43	감자	potato
4	가깝다	close	44	감자탕	Gamjatang, potato soup
5	가끔	sometimes	45	갑자기	suddenly
6	가다	go	46	값	price
7	가르치다	teach	47	강	river
8	가방	bag	48	강아지	puppy
9	가볍다	light	49	강좌	lecture
10	가수	singer	50	갖다	have
11	가슴	chest, breast	51	같다	same
12	가요	song	52	같이	together
13	가운데	middle	53	개	dog, ~ piece(s)
14	가위	scissors	54	개나리	forsythia
15	가을	autumn, fall	55	개인	individual
16	가장	most	56	거기	there
17	가져가다	take away	57	거리	street
18	가져오다	bring	58	거실	living room

19	가족	family	59	거울	mirror
20	가지	branch	60	거의	almost, nearly
21	가지다	have	61	거짓말	lie
22	각	each	62	걱정	anxiety, concern
23	간	while	63	걱정하다	worry
24	간단하다	simple, easy	64	건강	health
25	간단히	simply	65	건강하다	be healthy
26	간식	snack	66	건너가다	cross (a road)
27	간장	soy sauce	67	건너다	cross over
28	간호사	nurse	68	건너편	other side, opposite side
29	갈비	Galvi, spareribs	69	건물	building
30	갈비탕	Galbitang, spareribs soup	70	건배	cheers, toast
31	갈색	brown	71	걷다	walk
32	갈아타다	transfer	72	걸다	bet, call
33	감	persimmon	73	걸리다	get caught, take (time)
34	감기	cold	74	걸어가다	walk (go)

35	감기약	cold medicine	75	걸어오다	walk (come)
36	감다	close ~ (eyes)	76	검은색	black
37	감동	sensation	77	것	that thing, it
38	감동하다	be impressed	78	게임	game
39	감사	thank	79	겨울	winter
40	감사드립니다	thank you	80	겨울방학	winter vacation

No.	한글	English	No.	한글	English
81	결과	result	121	골목	alley
82	결정	decision	122	골프	golf
83	결정하다	decide	123	곱다	beautiful
84	결혼	marriage	124	곳	place
85	결혼식	wedding ceremony	125	공	ball
86	결혼하다	get married	126	공간	space
87	경기	competition, game	127	공기	air

88	경기장	stadium, arena	128	공무원	public official
89	경복궁	Gyeongbokgung	129	공부	study
90	경주	Gyeongju	130	공부하다	study
91	경찰	police	131	공연	show, public performance
92	경찰관	police officer	132	공원	park
93	경찰서	police office	133	공중전화	payphone, public phone
94	경치	view, landscape	134	공짜	free
95	경험	experience	135	공책	notebook, note
96	계단	stairs	136	공항	airport
97	계란	egg	137	공휴일	public holiday
98	계산하다	calculate	138	과	division
99	계속	continue	139	과거	past
100	계시다	be, exist (honorific form)	140	과일	fruit
101	계절	season	141	과자	snack

102	계획	plan	142	과학	science
103	고기	meat	143	관계	relation
104	고등학교	high school	144	관광하다	travel, sightsee
105	고등학생	high school student	145	관심	attention, interest
106	고르다	choose	146	광고	advertisement
107	고마웠습니다	Thank you (past tense)	147	괜찮다	be okay
108	고맙다	thank	148	괜찮습니다	It's fine.
109	고맙습니다	Thank you	149	교과서	textbook
110	고모	paternal aunt	150	교수	professor
111	고모부	paternal uncle	151	교실	classroom
112	고속버스	express bus	152	교체	substitute, change
113	고양이	cat	153	교통	traffic
114	고장	broken, malfunction	154	교통사고	traffic accident
115	고추	red pepper	155	교회	Church

116	고추장	Kochujang, red pepper paste	156	구	9
117	고치다	fix	157	구경하다	take a look
118	고프다	hungry	158	구두	shoes
119	고향	hometown	159	구름	cloud
120	곧	soon	160	구십	90

No.	한글	English	No.	한글	English
161	구월	September	201	그리고	and
162	구하다	save, seek, get	202	그리다	draw
163	국	soup	203	그림	drawing, picture
164	국내	domestic	204	그만	stop, finish
165	국립	national established, state	205	그분	his, the person
166	국수	noodle	206	그저께	day before yesterday
167	국어	Korean language	207	그중	among them
168	국적	nationality, country of citizenship	208	그쪽	there, the person

169	국제	International	209	그치다	stop, end, cease
170	군인	soldier, military personnel	210	극장	theatre, cinema
171	굽다	bake	211	근처	nearby, neighbourhood
172	권	~ book(s)	212	글	post, sentence, character
173	귀	ear	213	글쎄요	I do not know., well, I guess ~
174	귀엽다	cute	214	금방	soon, a little while ago
175	규칙	rule	215	금연	no smoking
176	귤	mandarin orange	216	금요일	Friday
177	그	it	217	금주	abstinence, temperance
178	그거	it	218	급	class, grade
179	그것	it	219	급하다	hurry, urgent

180	그곳	there	220	기간	term, period
181	그날	that day	221	기다리다	wait
182	그냥	just, as it is	222	기르다	cultivate, grow
183	그동안	meantime, meanwhile, up to now	223	기름	oil, gasoline
184	그들	them, they	224	기분	feeling
185	그때	then, at that time	225	기뻐하다	glad, delight
186	그래	Yes, Yeah	226	기쁘다	happy
187	그래서	so, thus	227	기사	article, driver, engineer
188	그램	gram	228	기숙사	dormitory
189	그러나	but, however	229	기억하다	remember
190	그러니까	so, because	230	기온	temperature
191	그러면	then, if so	231	기자	reporter
192	그런	then, such	232	기차	train
193	그런데	by the way, however	233	기침	cough
194	그럼	then	234	기타	other

No.	한글	English	No.	한글	English
195	그렇게	like that, so	235	긴장되다	be nervous
196	그렇구나	well, I see.	236	길	way, road
197	그렇다	Yes, that's it.	237	길다	long
198	그렇습니다	That's right.	238	김	seaweed
199	그렇지만	nevertheless, but	239	김밥	Kimbab
200	그릇	bowl, container, tableware	240	김치	Kimchi

No.	한글	English	No.	한글	English
241	김치찌개	Kimchi stew	281	남기다	leave
242	김포공항	Gimpo International Airport	282	남녀	men and women
243	까만색	black color	283	남대문시장	Namdaemun market
244	까맣다	black	284	남동생	younger brother
245	깎다	cut, shave	285	남미	South America

246	깜짝	startled, surprised	286	남북	north and south
247	깨끗하다	clean	287	남자	man
248	깨다	wake up, crack, break	288	남쪽	south
249	깨지다	chip, crack, break	289	남편	husband
250	꺼내다	take out	290	남학생	male student
251	껌	chewing gum	291	낮	day, noon, during the day
252	꼭	exactly, absolutely	292	낮다	low
253	꽃	flower	293	내	of mine, my
254	꽃집	florist	294	내가	I
255	꾸다	dream	295	내과	internal medicine
256	꿈	dream	296	내년	next year
257	끄다	turn off, extinguish, stop	297	내다	pay, put out
258	끓이다	boil	298	내려가다	go down
259	끝	end	299	내려오다	come down

260	끝나다	finish, end	300	내리다	go down
261	끝내다	finish	301	내용	content
262	끼다	put on, plug, (fog) rolls in	302	내일	tomorrow
263	나	I	303	냄비	pot
264	나가다	go out, get out	304	냄새	smell
265	나누다	Share, divide	305	냉면	cold noodle
266	나다	occur, come out	306	냉장고	refrigerator
267	나라	country	307	너	you
268	나무	tree	308	너무	too, very
269	나빠지다	spoil, deteriorate	309	넓다	wide
270	나쁘다	bad	310	넘다	exceed, more than
271	나오다	come out, appear	311	넘어지다	fall, fall
272	나이	age, old	312	넣다	put in
273	나중	later, after	313	네	yes, 4
274	나타나다	appear	314	넥타이	necktie
275	나흘	four days	315	넷	4

276	낚시	fishing	316	넷째	fourth
277	날	day	317	년	year
278	날씨	weather	318	노란색	yellow colour
279	날짜	date	319	노랗다	yellow
280	남	south, man	320	노래	song

No.	한글	English	No.	한글	English
321	노래방	Karaoke shop	361	다음달	next month
322	노래하다	sing	362	다음주	next week
323	노력하다	endeavour, strive	363	다음해	next year, the following year
324	노트	note	364	다이어트	diet
325	녹색	green	365	다치다	hurt
326	녹차	green tea	366	닦다	wipe, polish
327	놀다	play	367	단어	word
328	놀라다	be surprised	368	단점	the disadvantages, shortcomings, anddrawbacks
329	농구	basketball	369	닫다	close

330	높다	high	370	닫히다	shut, close
331	놓다	put	371	달	month, moon
332	누가	who	372	달걀	egg
333	누구	who	373	달다	sweet
334	누나	sister (as seen by the younger brother)	374	달러	dollar
335	누르다	press down, push	375	달력	calendar
336	눈	eye, snow	376	달리다	run
337	눈물	tear	377	닭	chicken, hen
338	눈사람	snowman	378	닭고기	chicken
339	눈싸움	staring contest, snowball fight	379	닮다	resemble
340	눕다	lie down, sleep	380	담그다	dip, pickle
341	뉴스	news	381	담배	tobacco
342	뉴욕	New York	382	답장	reply
343	느끼다	feel	383	당근	carrot
344	느낌	feeling	384	당신	you
345	느리다	slow	385	대	versus, large

346	늘	always	386	대답	answer
347	늘다	gain, increase	387	대답하다	answer, reply
348	능력	ability	388	대부분	mostly, almost
349	늦다	late, delay	389	대사관	embassy
350	늦잠	overslept, sleeping in late	390	대학	university, college
351	님	Sir	391	대학교	university, college
352	다	all, whole	392	대학생	college student
353	다녀오다	return, come back	393	대학원	graduate school
354	다니다	go, commute	394	대학원생	postgraduate student, graduate student
355	다르다	different	395	대한민국	Republic of Korea, South Korea
356	다른	other ~, another ~, different ~	396	대화	conversation, dialogue
357	다리	bridge, leg, foot	397	대회	competition, tournament
358	다섯	5	398	댁	house
359	다시	again	399	더	more

360	다음	next, after	400	더럽다	dirty

No.	한글	English	No.	한글	English
401	더운물	hot water	441	두부	tofu
402	덕분	thanks for, thanks to	442	두부찌개	tofu soup
403	덥다	hot	443	둘	2
404	덮다	cover	444	둘째	second, the second of~
405	데리다	bring, take along	445	뒤	rear, back
406	데이트	date, dating	446	뒤쪽	behind, back, towards the rear
407	도로	road	447	드라마	drama
408	도서관	library	448	드리다	give
409	도시	City	449	드시다	eat (honorific form)
410	도와주다	help	450	듣기	listening, hearing
411	도움	help, assistance	451	듣다	listen

412	도착	arrival	452	들	field, ~s,
413	도착하다	arrive	453	들다	hold, enter
414	도쿄	Tokyo	454	들어가다	go in, enter
415	독서	reading	455	들어오다	come in, enter
416	독서실	reading room	456	등	etc, back
417	독서하다	read	457	등산	hiking, mountain-climbing
418	독일	Germany	458	등산복	mountaineering clothing
419	돈	money	459	등산화	hiking boots, climbing shoes
420	돌아가다	return, go back	460	디브이디	DVD
421	돌아오다	come back, come home	461	디자인	design
422	돕다	help	462	따뜻하다	warm
423	동네	town, neighbourhood	463	따라가다	follow
424	동대문시장	Dongdaemun market	464	따라오다	come with, follow

425	동물	animal	465	따로	separately
426	동생	brother, sister	466	따르다	follow
427	동아리	club, group	467	딸	daughter
428	동안	during, between	468	딸기	strawberry
429	동양	eastern, orient	469	땀	sweat
430	동전	coin	470	때	time
431	동쪽	east	471	때문	because, for ~, so~
432	돼지	pig	472	떠나다	leave
433	돼지고기	pork	473	떠들다	chatter, make a noise
434	되다	become	474	떡	rice cake
435	된장	fermented soybean paste	475	떡국	rice cake soup
436	된장국	soybean paste soup	476	떡볶이	Toppogi
437	된장찌개	soybean paste stew	477	떨어지다	drop
438	두	two	478	또	in addition, again

439	두껍다	thick	479	또는	or
440	두다	put	480	똑같다	same

No.	한글	English	No.	한글	English
481	똑바로	upright, straight	521	매다	tie
482	뛰다	run	522	매우	extremely, very
483	뜨겁다	hot	523	매일	everyday
484	뜨다	rise, open (the eyes)	524	매주	every week
485	뜻	meaning	525	맥주	beer
486	라디오	radio	526	맵다	spicy
487	라면	ramen	527	머리	head, hair
488	러시아	Russia	528	먹다	eat
489	로션	skin lotion	529	먼저	first, first of all, before
490	마늘	garlic	530	멀다	far, distant, long
491	마르다	dry	531	멋있다	cool, nice
492	마리	~ animal(s), ~ head(s)	532	메뉴	menu

493	마시다	drink	533	메다	shoulder, carry
494	마음	mind, feeling	534	메모	memo
495	마지막	last	535	메시지	message
496	마치다	finish, end	536	멕시코	Mexico
497	마흔	40	537	며칠	a few days, what date
498	막히다	be blocked, be clogged	538	면도	razor, shaving
499	만	only, ten thousand	539	명	~ person(s)
500	만나다	meet	540	명절	holidays, annual events
501	만두	dumpling	541	몇	a few, several
502	만들다	make, create	542	모두	all, everyone
503	만일	if, should	543	모레	the day after tomorrow
504	만지다	touch	544	모르겠습니다	I don't know.
505	만화	comic book, cartoon	545	모르다	do not know

506	많다	many	546	모시다	take you, serve you (honorific form)
507	많이	a lot of, many	547	모양	shape, form, style
508	말	word, talk	548	모으다	collect, gather
509	말씀	words, remarks	549	모이다	gather, get together
510	말씀하다	talk	550	모임	meeting, gathering
511	말하기	speaking	551	모자	hat
512	말하다	say, talk	552	목	neck, throat
513	맑다	clear, clean	553	목걸이	necklace
514	맛	flavour, taste	554	목소리	voice
515	맛없다	not delicious	555	목요일	Thursday
516	맛있다	delicious	556	목욕	bath, bathing
517	맞다	right, fit, correct	557	목욕하다	take a bath
518	맞습니다	That's right.	558	목적	purpose
519	맞아요	That's right.	559	몸	body
520	맞은편	across, the other side, opposite	560	몸살	sickness, a disease that comes from fatigue

No.	한글	English	No.	한글	English
561	못하다	~ can not do	601	바뀌다	be changed
562	몽골	Mongolia	602	바나나	banana
563	무	radish	603	바다	sea
564	무겁다	heavy	604	바닷가	beach
565	무궁화	rose of Sharon	605	바라다	hope
566	무료	free	606	바람	wind
567	무릎	knee	607	바로	immediately, soon, just
568	무리	swarm, unreasonable	608	바르다	right, paint, wear
569	무섭다	scary	609	바쁘다	busy
570	무슨	what	610	바이올린	violin
571	무엇	what	611	바지	pants
572	무엇이	what	612	박물관	museum
573	무역	trade	613	박수	clap, applause
574	무용	dance	614	밖	out, outside
575	무척	very	615	반	half, group
576	문	door, gate	616	반갑다	nice to meet, happy

577	문구점	stationery store	617	반갑습니다	Nice to meet you.
578	문장	sentence	618	반년	half a year
579	문제	problem	619	반달	half-moon
580	문화	culture	620	반바지	shorts
581	묻다	ask	621	반지	ring
582	물	water	622	반찬	side dish
583	물건	stuff, thing	623	받다	receive
584	물론	sure, of course	624	발	foot, leg
585	물어보다	ask	625	발가락	toe(s)
586	뭐	what	626	발음	pronunciation
587	미국	The United States	627	발전	development
588	미래	future	628	발표	announcement, presentation
589	미리	in advance, beforehand	629	밝다	bright
590	미술	art	630	밤	night
591	미술관	art gallery, art museum	631	밥	rice, meal
592	미안하다	sorry	632	방	room

593	미안합니다	I'm sorry.	633	방법	way, method
594	미용실	beauty salon	634	방송	broadcast
595	미터	meter	635	방송국	broadcast stations
596	민속촌	folk village	636	방학	vacation
597	밀가루	flour	637	배	ship, stomach, pear
598	밀리다	be shaved, be pushed	638	배고프다	hungry
599	밑	bottom, below	639	배구	volleyball
600	바꾸다	change	640	배달	delivery

No.	한글	English	No.	한글	English
641	배부르다	be full (I am full.)	681	부부	the couple, husband and wife, a married couple
642	배우	actor	682	부산	Busan
643	배우다	learn	683	부업	sideline
644	배탈	stomachache	684	부엌	kitchen
645	백	100	685	부인	wife, Mrs.
646	백화점	department store	686	부장	director

647	버리다	abandon, throw away	687	부지런하다	diligent
648	버스	bus	688	부치다	send, fry, transmit
649	번	~ time(s)	689	부탁	request, please
650	번호	number	690	부탁하다	beg, ask
651	벌다	earn, make money	691	북쪽	North
652	벌써	already	692	분	~ person(s), ~ minute(s)
653	벗다	take-off (clothes, shoes)	693	분위기	#N/A
654	벚꽃	cherry blossom	694	불	fire, electrical light
655	베이징	Beijing	695	불고기	Bulgogi, grilled meat
656	베트남	Vietnam	696	불다	blow (wind or whistle, musical instruments, etc.)
657	벽	wall	697	불편하다	uncomfortable, inconvenient
658	변호사	lawyer	698	붓다	pour

659	별	star	699	붙다	stick, pass a test
660	별로	not really	700	붙이다	attach, stick
661	병	illness, ~ bottle(s)	701	브라질	Brazil
662	병원	hospital	702	블라우스	blouse
663	보내다	send, spend	703	비	rain
664	보다	see	704	비누	soap
665	보도	sidewalk, report	705	비디오	video
666	보이다	show, look	706	비밀	secret
667	보통	usually, normally, in general	707	비빔밥	Bibimbap, mixed rice
668	복숭아	peach	708	비슷하다	similar, like
669	복잡하다	complicated, crowded	709	비싸다	expensive
670	볶다	fry	710	비행기	airplane
671	볶음밥	fried rice	711	비행장	airfield, airport
672	볼펜	ballpoint pen	712	빌딩	building

673	봄	spring	713	빌리다	borrow, lend
674	봉지	bag	714	빠르다	fast
675	봉투	envelope	715	빨간색	red colour
676	뵙다	meet	716	빨갛다	red
677	부동산	real estate	717	빨다	suck, do laundry
678	부드럽다	soft, friendly	718	빨래	laundry, wash
679	부르다	call, sing	719	빨리	quickly
680	부모	parents	720	빵	bread

No.	한글	English	No.	한글	English
721	빵집	bakery	761	삼촌	paternal uncle
722	빼다	remove, pull, pull out	762	상관	relation
723	뿐	only	763	상자	box
724	사	4	764	상처	wound, scratch
725	사거리	intersection, four corners	765	상품	product
726	사계절	four seasons	766	새	bird, new

727	사고	accident	767	새로	newly
728	사과	apple	768	새벽	dawn, late at night, early morning
729	사다	buy	769	새우	shrimp
730	사람	person, man	770	색	color
731	사랑	love	771	색깔	color
732	사랑하다	love	772	샌드위치	sandwich
733	사례	case, example	773	생각	thinking thought
734	사무실	office	774	생각되다	be considered, it seems~
735	사물	object, thing	775	생각하다	think
736	사십	40	776	생기다	form, arise
737	사업가	entrepreneur, businessman	777	생선	fish
738	사용하다	use	778	생신	birthday (honorific form)
739	사원	temple, employee	779	생일	birthday
740	사월	April	780	생활	life

741	사이	between, while	781	샤워하다	take a shower
742	사이다	cider	782	샴푸	shampoo
743	사이즈	size	783	서다	stand
744	사인하다	sign	784	서로	each other, both
745	사장	CEO, the president	785	서류	document
746	사전	dictionary	786	서른	30
747	사진	picture, photo	787	서비스	service
748	사진기	camera	788	서양	western, west
749	사촌	cousin	789	서울	Seoul
750	사탕	candy	790	서울역	Seoul station
751	사흘	3 days	791	서점	bookstore
752	산	mountain	792	서쪽	west, western
753	산책	walk	793	선물	gift, present
754	살	flesh, ~ year(s) old	794	선배	elder, senior
755	살다	live	795	선생님	teacher
756	삼	3	796	선수	player

757	삼거리	intersection, three-way intersection	797	선택하다	choose, select
758	삼계탕	Samgyetang	798	선풍기	fan
759	삼십	30	799	설거지	washing dishes, dish-washing
760	삼월	March	800	설날	Lunar New Year

No.	한글	English	No.	한글	English
801	설렁탕	Seolleongtang	841	수도	capital, water supply
802	설명	explanation, description	842	수돗물	tap water
803	설명하다	explain	843	수박	watermelon
804	설악산	Mt. Seorak	844	수술하다	operate on for
805	설탕	sugar	845	수업	class, lesson
806	섬	island	846	수영	swimming
807	성	castle, last name	847	수영복	swimsuit

808	성격	personality	848	수영장	swimming pool
809	성함	name	849	수요일	Wednesday
810	세계	world	850	수저	chopsticks and a spoon
811	세수하다	wash	851	수첩	note, notebook
812	세우다	set up, formulate	852	수학	mathematics
813	세일하다	have a sale	853	숙제	homework
814	세탁기	washing machine	854	순서	order, turn
815	세탁소	dry cleaners, laundromat	855	숟가락	spoon
816	센터	centre	856	술	alcohol, liquor
817	센티미터	centimeter	857	쉬다	rest
818	셋	3	858	쉰	50
819	셋째	third	859	쉽다	easy
820	소	small, cow	860	슈퍼마켓	supermarket
821	소개	introduction	861	스물	20

822	소개하다	introduce	862	스웨터	sweater
823	소고기	beef	863	스케이트	skate
824	소금	salt	864	스키	ski, skiing
825	소리	sound, voice	865	스키장	ski resort
826	소설	novel	866	스타	star
827	소설가	novelist	867	스타킹	stockings
828	소식	news	868	스트레스	stress
829	소파	sofa	869	스페인어	Spanish
830	소포	parcel	870	스포츠	sport
831	소풍	picnic, trip	871	슬퍼하다	sorrow, mourn
832	소화제	peptic, digestive	872	슬프다	sad
833	속	inside	873	습관	habit
834	손	hand	874	시	city, time
835	손가락	finger	875	시간	time
836	손님	customer	876	시간표	schedule, timetable
837	손수건	handkerchief	877	시계	clock
838	송이	bunch, flower, cluster	878	시골	countryside

839	쇼핑	shopping	879	시끄럽다	noisy
840	수건	towel, washcloth	880	시내	downtown, city, stream

No.	한글	English	No.	한글	English
881	시다	sour	921	쓰기	writing, dictation
882	시디	CD	922	쓰다	write, use, wear (glasses)
883	시민	citizen	923	쓰레기	garbage
884	시설	facility	924	쓰이다	be written, be used
885	시외	suburbs	925	씨	seed, Mr. ~
886	시원하다	cool, refresh	926	씩	each, every, per
887	시월	October	927	씹다	chew, bite
888	시작	start	928	씻다	wash
889	시작되다	begin	929	아가씨	Miss, daughter
890	시작하다	start, begin	930	아기	baby, toddler

891	시장	market	931	아까	a, while ago
892	시청	city hall	932	아내	wife
893	시키다	make someone do it, order	933	아뇨	no
894	시험	exam, test	934	아니다	no
895	식당	restaurant, cafeteria	935	아니오	no
896	식사	meal	936	아니요	no
897	식탁	table	937	아들	son
898	신	god, new	938	아랍어	Arabic
899	신다	put on, wear	939	아래	bottom, under
900	신문	newspaper	940	아름답다	beautiful
901	신발	shoes, footwear	941	아마	maybe, perhaps
902	신청서	application forms	942	아무	any
903	신청하다	put in for, apply for	943	아버님	father
904	실례	excuse	944	아버지	father
905	실례하다	be excused	945	아빠	dad
906	실수	mistake, failure	946	아시아	Asia

907	싫다	hate	947	아이	child
908	싫어하다	dislike, hate	948	아이스크림	ice cream
909	심하다	severe, terrible	949	아저씨	uncle, mister
910	십	10	950	아주	very, completely
911	십이월	December	951	아주머니	old lady, madame, aunt
912	십일월	November	952	아줌마	old lady, madame, aunt
913	싱겁다	not salty	953	아직	yet, still
914	싶다	want	954	아침	morning, breakfast
915	싸다	cheap, wrap	955	아침밥	breakfast
916	싸우다	fight	956	아침식사	breakfast
917	쌀	rice	957	아파트	apartment, mansion
918	쌀밥	cooked rice	958	아프다	painful, sick
919	쌓이다	stack up, pile up	959	아프리카	Africa
920	썰다	chop, cut	960	아홉	9

No.	한글	English	No.	한글	English
961	아흔	90	1001	어른	adult
962	악기	musical instrument	1002	어리다	young
963	안	within, not ~	1003	어린이	child
964	안경	glasses	1004	어머	oh, well
965	안내하다	guide, invite	1005	어머니	mother
966	안녕하세요	hi, hello	1006	어머님	mother
967	안녕하십니까	hello	1007	어서	hurry, quickly
968	안다	embrace, cradle	1008	어울리다	look good on, befit
969	안전하다	safe	1009	어저께	yesterday
970	앉다	sit	1010	어제	yesterday
971	알다	know	1011	어젯밤	last night
972	알리다	inform	1012	언니	sister (as seen from the younger sister)
973	알맞다	fit, appropriate	1013	언제	when

974	알았습니다	I understood.	1014	언제나	always, anytime
975	앞	front, previous	1015	얼굴	face
976	애	child	1016	얼마나	how much
977	액세서리	accessory	1017	얼음	ice
978	야구	baseball	1018	엄마	mom
979	야채	vegetable	1019	없다	none, no, not
980	약	about, medicine	1020	없이	without
981	약간	slightly, a little	1021	에어컨	air conditioner
982	약국	pharmacy	1022	엔	yen
983	약사	pharmacist	1023	엘리베이터	elevator
984	약속	appointment, promise	1024	여권	passport
985	얇다	thin	1025	여기	here
986	양	amount, sheep	1026	여기저기	here and there
987	양말	socks	1027	여덟	8

988	양복	suit	1028	여동생	younger sister
989	양식	form, western style	1029	여든	80
990	양파	onion	1030	여러	various, many
991	얘기하다	talk	1031	여러가지	several, various
992	어깨	shoulder	1032	여러분	everyone, ladies and gentlemen
993	어느	which, how	1033	여름	summer
994	어둡다	dark	1034	여보세요	hello
995	어디	where	1035	여섯	6
996	어떤	which, what	1036	여자	woman
997	어떻게	how	1037	여학생	female student
998	어떻다	how	1038	여행	travel
999	어떻습니까?	How is it?	1039	여행사	travel agency, travel firm
1000	어렵다	difficult	1040	역	station

No.	한글	English	No.	한글	English

1041	역사	history	1081	오랫동안	for a long time
1042	연락처	contact information	1082	오렌지	orange
1043	연세	age (honorific form)	1083	오르다	climb
1044	연습	practice	1084	오른쪽	right side, right
1045	연습하다	practice	1085	오리	duck
1046	연예인	celebrity	1086	오빠	brother (as seen by the younger sister)
1047	연필	pencil	1087	오십	50
1048	연휴	consecutive holidays	1088	오월	May
1049	열	10	1089	오이	cucumber
1050	열다	open	1090	오전	morning, a.m.
1051	열리다	be opened	1091	오징어	squid
1052	열쇠	key	1092	오후	afternoon
1053	열심히	hard, enthusiastic	1093	올라가다	go up
1054	열차	train	1094	올라오다	come up
1055	엽서	postcard	1095	올려놓다	put on, place

1056	영	spirit, zero	1096	올림픽	Olympics
1057	영국	The United Kingdom	1097	올해	this year
1058	영상	video	1098	옮기다	move, transfer, translate
1059	영어	English	1099	옷	dress, clothes
1060	영어회화	English conversation	1100	옷가게	clothing store
1061	영하	minus, below zero	1101	옷장	closet
1062	영화	movie	1102	와이셔츠	shirt
1063	영화관	movie theater	1103	왜	why
1064	영화배우	movie star	1104	왜냐하면	because
1065	영화표	movie ticket	1105	외국	foreign country
1066	옆	side	1106	외국어	foreign language
1067	예	yes	1107	외국인	foreigner
1068	예문	example, model sentence	1108	외롭다	lonely
1069	예쁘다	pretty, beautiful	1109	외삼촌	maternal uncle

1070	예순	60	1110	외숙모	maternal aunt
1071	예약	reservation	1111	외출하다	go out
1072	옛날	a long ago, olden days	1112	외할머니	maternal grandmother
1073	오	5	1113	외할아버지	maternal grandfather
1074	오늘	today	1114	왼쪽	left
1075	오다	come	1115	요금	fee
1076	오래	long, much	1116	요르단	Jordan
1077	오래간만	after a long time	1117	요리	cooking, cuisine
1078	오래간만입니다	Long time no see.	1118	요일	day of the week
1079	오랜만	after a long time	1119	요즘	nowadays, around this time, lately
1080	오랜만에	after a long time	1120	우리	we, us

No.	한글	English	No.	한글	English
1121	우리나라	our country, South Korea	1161	은행	bank

1122	우산	umbrella	1162	은행원	bank clerk
1123	우선	first	1163	음료수	drink, soft drink
1124	우유	milk	1164	음반	record
1125	우체국	post office	1165	음식	food, cooking
1126	우표	stamp	1166	음악	music
1127	운동	exercise	1167	음악가	musician
1128	운동복	sportswear, gym clothes	1168	응	Yeah (answer)
1129	운동선수	athlete	1169	의미	meaning
1130	운동장	playground, athletic field	1170	의사	doctor
1131	운동하다	exercise	1171	의자	chair
1132	운동화	sports shoes	1172	이	this, tooth, 2
1133	운전하다	drive	1173	이거	this
1134	울다	cry	1174	이것	this
1135	울리다	make cry, chime	1175	이곳	this place, here
1136	움직이다	move	1176	이따가	later
1137	웃기다	funny, make	1177	이런	this, such ~

		someone laugh			
1138	웃다	laugh	1178	이렇게	like this, so, in this way
1139	원	won (currency units of Korea)	1179	이렇다	like this
1140	원피스	one-piece dress	1180	이름	name
1141	원하다	want, wish, desire	1181	이메일	e-mail
1142	월	month	1182	이모	maternal aunt
1143	월급	monthly salary	1183	이모부	maternal uncle
1144	월드컵	world cup	1184	이번	this time
1145	월세	monthly rent	1185	이분	this person
1146	월요일	Monday	1186	이사	move, moving
1147	웬일	for some reason, What was it?	1187	이상	more than, strange
1148	위	top, up	1188	이상하다	strange, funny, weird
1149	위치	location, position	1189	이십	20

No.	한글	English	No.	한글	English
1150	위하다	for, in favour of, for the sake of	1190	이야기	story
1151	위험하다	dangerous	1191	이야기하다	talk
1152	유럽	Europe	1192	이용	usage
1153	유리	glass	1193	이용하다	use
1154	유명하다	famous	1194	이월	February
1155	유월	June	1195	이유	reason
1156	유학	study abroad	1196	이제	now
1157	유학생	foreign student, international student	1197	이집트	Egypt
1158	유행	trend	1198	이쪽	this way, here, this person
1159	육	6	1199	이틀	two days
1160	육십	60	1200	이해	understanding

No.	한글	English	No.	한글	English
1201	이해하다	understand	1241	입다	put on, wear

1202	인	sign, ~ person(s)	1242	입원하다	hospitalize
1203	인구	population	1243	입학	admission
1204	인기	popularity	1244	있다	have, there
1205	인기스타	popular star	1245	잊다	forget
1206	인도	India	1246	잊어버리다	forget
1207	인사	greetings	1247	자	character, Here we go.
1208	인사하다	greet	1248	자기	myself, own
1209	인삼	ginseng	1249	자다	sleep
1210	인상	impression	1250	자동차	car, automobile
1211	인천	Incheon	1251	자동차회사	car company
1212	인터넷	internet	1252	자료	material, document
1213	인터뷰하다	interview	1253	자르다	cut
1214	인형	doll	1254	자리	seat, location
1215	일	work, 1, day	1255	자신	myself, own

1216	일곱	7	1256	자연	nature
1217	일기	diary	1257	자유	freedom
1218	일기예보	weather forecast	1258	자장면	Jajangmyeon
1219	일본	Japan	1259	자전거	bicycle
1220	일본드라마	Japanese drama	1260	자주	often
1221	일본말	Japanese language	1261	작년	last year
1222	일본사람	Japanese people	1262	작다	small
1223	일본어	Japanese language	1263	작은아버지	uncle
1224	일본요리	Japanese food	1264	작은어머니	aunt
1225	일상생활	everyday life	1265	잔	glass, cup(s)
1226	일식	Japanese style, Japanese food	1266	잔치	party, feast
1227	일어나다	rise, stand, occur	1267	잘	well
1228	일어서다	get up, stand up	1268	잘못	mistake
1229	일요일	Sunday	1269	잘생기다	handsome

No.	한글	English	No.	한글	English
1230	일월	January	1270	잘하다	do well, good at
1231	일주일	one week	1271	잠	slumbers, sleep
1232	일찍	early	1272	잠깐	for a while, a little
1233	일하다	work	1273	잠시	for a bit, for a while, a little
1234	일흔	70	1274	잠자다	sleep, go to bed
1235	읽기	reading	1275	잡다	catch, grab, hold
1236	읽다	read	1276	잡수시다	eat (honorific form)
1237	잃다	lose	1277	잡지	magazine
1238	잃어버리다	lose	1278	장	~ chapter(s), ~ sheet(s)
1239	입	mouth	1279	장갑	gloves
1240	입구	entrance	1280	장마	rainy season

No.	한글	English	No.	한글	English
1281	장마철	rainy season	1321	젓가락	chopsticks

1282	장미	rose	1322	정거장	station, depot
1283	장소	place	1323	정도	degree
1284	장점	advantage	1324	정류장	station, bus stop
1285	재료	material	1325	정리하다	straighten out, organize
1286	재미없다	not funny, uninteresting	1326	정말	truly
1287	재미있다	interesting	1327	정문	front door, main gate
1288	재킷	jacket	1328	정보	information
1289	저	that	1329	정하다	choose, establish
1290	저거	that	1330	제가	I
1291	저것	that	1331	제목	title
1292	저곳	over there	1332	제일	most
1293	저기	there, over there	1333	제주도	Jeju Island
1294	저녁	dinner, evening, night	1334	조금	a little
1295	저녁식사	dinner	1335	조사하다	investigate

1296	저렇게	like that, in that way	1336	조선	shipbuilding, Korea
1297	저분	that person	1337	조선말	Korean language
1298	저쪽	there, over there	1338	조선어	Korean language
1299	저희	we	1339	조심하다	be careful, warn
1300	적	enemy	1340	조용하다	silent, quiet
1301	적다	be few, write down	1341	조용히	quietly
1302	전	all, before	1342	조카	nephew
1303	전공	major	1343	졸업	graduation
1304	전기자동차	electric car	1344	졸업하다	graduate
1305	전자사전	electronic dictionary	1345	좀	a little
1306	전하다	tell	1346	좀더	a little more
1307	전혀	not at all	1347	좁다	narrow
1308	전화	telephone	1348	종로	Jong-ro
1309	전화기	telephone	1349	종류	kind, type
1310	전화번호	phone number	1350	종업원	employee

No.	한글	English	No.	한글	English
1311	절	~ section(s), temple	1351	종이	paper
1312	절대	never, absolutely	1352	종일	all-day
1313	젊다	young	1353	좋다	good
1314	점	point	1354	좋아하다	like
1315	점수	score, point	1355	죄송하다	sorry
1316	점심	lunch	1356	주	week
1317	점심시간	lunchtime	1357	주다	give
1318	점심식사	lunch	1358	주로	mainly
1319	점원	clerk	1359	주말	weekend
1320	점퍼	jacket	1360	주머니	pocket, pouch

No.	한글	English	No.	한글	English
1361	주무시다	sleep, rest	1401	지다	lose
1362	주문하다	order	1402	지도	map
1363	주변	around	1403	지방	fat, region
1364	주부	housewife	1404	지우개	eraser
1365	주사	injection	1405	지키다	protect

No.	Korean	English	No.	Korean	English
1366	주소	address	1406	지하	underground
1367	주스	juice	1407	지하도	underpass
1368	주위	around	1408	지하철	subway
1369	주인	owner	1409	지하철역	subway station
1370	주차장	parking lot	1410	직업	job, profession
1371	주차하다	park	1411	직원	employee, staff
1372	주황색	orange colour	1412	직장	workplace
1373	죽	bamboo, porridge	1413	직접	directly, direct
1374	죽다	die	1414	진달래	azalea
1375	준비	preparation	1415	질	quality
1376	준비하다	prepare	1416	질문	question
1377	줄	line, column, string	1417	질문하다	ask a question
1378	줄다	shrink, decrease	1418	짐	load, baggage
1379	중	medium, during	1419	집	house, shop
1380	중국	China	1420	짓다	build, create

1381	중국어	Chinese	1421	짜다	salty, make (the plan)
1382	중국집	Chinese restaurant	1422	짜리	a value (won coin)
1383	중식	Chinese cuisine	1423	짧다	short
1384	중심	center	1424	쪽	side, page
1385	중요	importance	1425	쯤	about, around ~
1386	중요하다	important	1426	찌개	stew, soup
1387	중학교	middle school, Junior high school	1427	찍다	pierce, take (a photo), press
1388	중학생	middle school student	1428	차	car, tea
1389	즐거워하다	have fun	1429	차갑다	cold
1390	즐겁다	fun, be pleasant	1430	차다	kick
1391	즐기다	enjoy, have fun	1431	차리다	prepare, arrange
1392	증세	symptom, medical condition	1432	착하다	be good, friendly
1393	지각	tardy, being late	1433	참	very
1394	지갑	wallet	1434	창문	window

No.	한글	English	No.	한글	English
1395	지금	now	1435	찾다	find, visit
1396	지나다	pass by	1436	찾아가다	go to visit
1397	지난달	last month	1437	찾아오다	come to visit
1398	지난번	last time	1438	채소	vegetable
1399	지난주	last week	1439	책	book
1400	지내다	stay, spend, live	1440	책방	bookstore

No.	한글	English	No.	한글	English
1441	책상	desk	1481	층	layer, ~ floor
1442	책임	responsibility	1482	치과	dentist, dentistry
1443	책장	bookshelf	1483	치료하다	treat
1444	처음	first, for the first time	1484	치마	skirt
1445	처음 뵙겠습니다	Nice to meet you.	1485	치약	toothpaste
1446	천	1000	1486	친구	friend

1447	천천히	slowly	1487	친절하다	be kind
1448	철	iron, season	1488	친척	relative
1449	첫	first	1489	친하다	close, familiar
1450	첫째	first	1490	칠	7
1451	청바지	blue jeans	1491	칠십	70
1452	청소기	vacuum cleaner	1492	칠월	July
1453	청소하다	sweep, clean	1493	칠판	blackboard
1454	초	~second(s)	1494	침대	bed
1455	초대하다	invite	1495	칫솔	toothbrush
1456	초등학교	elementary school	1496	카드	card
1457	초등학생	elementary student	1497	카레	curry
1458	초록색	green colour	1498	카메라	camera
1459	초콜릿	chocolate	1499	카페	cafe, coffee shops
1460	촬영하다	take a picture	1500	칼	knife, cutlery, swords
1461	최고	best, the highest	1501	캐나다	Canada

1462	추다	dance	1502	커피	coffee
1463	추석	Chusoku (Korean Thanksgiving Day)	1503	커피숍	coffee shop
1464	추억	memory	1504	컴퓨터	computer, PC
1465	축구	football, soccer	1505	컵	cup
1466	축제	festival	1506	케이크	cake
1467	축하	celebration	1507	켜다	turn on (the light, the power, etc.)
1468	축하하다	celebrate	1508	코	nose
1469	축하합니다	congratulations	1509	코트	coat
1470	출구	exit	1510	코피	nosebleed
1471	출근하다	go to work	1511	콜라	Coke
1472	출발	start, departure	1512	콧노래	humming
1473	출발하다	depart	1513	콧물	snot, nasal discharge
1474	출장	business trip	1514	콩	bean, soy
1475	춤	dance	1515	크기	size
1476	춤추다	dance	1516	크다	big, large

1477	춥다	cold	1517	크리스마스	Christmas
1478	취미	hobby	1518	큰아버지	uncle
1479	취소하다	cancel	1519	큰어머니	aunt
1480	취직하다	get a job	1520	키	key, height

No.	한글	English	No.	한글	English
1521	킬로그램	kilogram	1561	펜	pen
1522	킬로미터	kilometer	1562	펴다	spread, stretch
1523	타다	ride, get on	1563	편	side, episode
1524	타월	towel	1564	편지	letter
1525	탁구	table tennis	1565	편하다	comfortable, easy, convenient
1526	태국	Thailand	1566	평양	Pyongyang
1527	태권도	Taekwondo	1567	평일	weekday
1528	태어나다	be born	1568	포도	grape
1529	태풍	typhoon	1569	포장	packing
1530	택시	taxi	1570	표	table, ticket

1531	탤런트	entertainers	1571	표현	expression
1532	터미널	terminal	1572	푹	deeply
1533	테니스	tennis	1573	풀	pool, grass
1534	테이블	table	1574	풀다	solve
1535	텔레비전	TV	1575	프랑스	France
1536	토마토	tomato	1576	프로그램	program
1537	토요일	Saturday	1577	프린트	print
1538	통	barrel, ~ package(s)	1578	피	blood
1539	통장	bank book, (deposit) passbook	1579	피곤하다	tired
1540	통하다	pass, lead	1580	피다	bloom
1541	퇴근하다	leave the office	1581	피아노	piano
1542	특별히	especially	1582	피우다	smoke, bloom
1543	특징	characteristic, feature	1583	피자	pizza
1544	특히	especially, in particular	1584	필름	film
1545	틀다	turn on (the switch)	1585	필요	necessity
1546	틀리다	wrong	1586	필요하다	need

No.	한글	English	No.	한글	English
1547	티셔츠	t-shirt	1587	필통	pencil case
1548	팀	team	1588	하나	1
1549	파	wave, green onion	1589	하늘	sky
1550	파란색	blue colour	1590	하늘색	sky blue, light blue
1551	파랗다	blue	1591	하다	do, say
1552	파티	party	1592	하루	one day
1553	팔	8	1593	하숙	boarding house, lodging house
1554	팔다	sell	1594	하숙집	boarding house, lodging house
1555	팔리다	sell, be sold	1595	하얀색	white colour
1556	팔십	80	1596	하얗다	white
1557	팔월	August	1597	하지만	but, however
1558	패션	fashion	1598	학	crane
1559	퍼센트	percent	1599	학교	school
1560	페이지	page	1600	학기	semester

No.	한글	English	No.	한글	English
1601	학년	grade, school year	1641	호주	Australia

1602	학생	student	1642	호텔	hotel
1603	학생증	student ID card	1643	혼자	alone
1604	학원	academy, school	1644	홈페이지	home page
1605	한	one, one of the ~	1645	홍차	black tea
1606	한강	Han River, Hangang	1646	화	anger
1607	한국	Korea	1647	화가	artist, painter
1608	한국드라마	Korean Drama	1648	화나다	angry
1609	한국말	Korean language	1649	화내다	get angry
1610	한국사람	Korean people	1650	화요일	Tuesday
1611	한국어	Korean language	1651	화장실	restroom, toilet, lavatory
1612	한국요리	Korean cuisine	1652	화장품	cosmetics
1613	한글	Hangul	1653	화장하다	makeup
1614	한번	once	1654	확인하다	confirm, check

1615	한복	Hanbok, Korean traditional clothes	1655	환영하다	Welcome
1616	한식	Korean cuisine	1656	환자	patient
1617	한자	Chinese character	1657	회사	company
1618	할머니	grandmother	1658	회사원	employee
1619	할아버지	grandfather	1659	회색	grey
1620	할인	sale, discount	1660	회의	conference
1621	함께	together	1661	횡단보도	crosswalk
1622	합격	pass	1662	후	after
1623	항상	always	1663	후배	Junior
1624	해	year, sun	1664	휴가	vacation, holiday
1625	해외	overseas	1665	휴대전화	cell phone, mobile phone
1626	해외여행	overseas trip	1666	휴일	holiday
1627	핸드폰	cell phone, mobile phone	1667	휴지	toilet paper
1628	햄버거	hamburger	1668	휴지통	trash can

1629	햇빛	sunshine, sunlight	1669	흐리다	cloudy
1630	행복	happiness	1670	흰색	white colour
1631	행복하다	happy	1671	힘	power
1632	행사	event	1672	형제	Sibling
1633	허리	waist, hip			
1634	현금	cash			
1635	현재	now, current			
1636	형	brother (as seen by the younger brother)			
1637	형님	big brother (honorific form)			

4. PRACTICE MAKES PERFECT

Welcome to the heart of your language learning journey – the practice phase. In this chapter, we'lldelve into the importance of consistent practice and provide you with effective strategies to sharpen your skills for the TOPIK 1 exam.

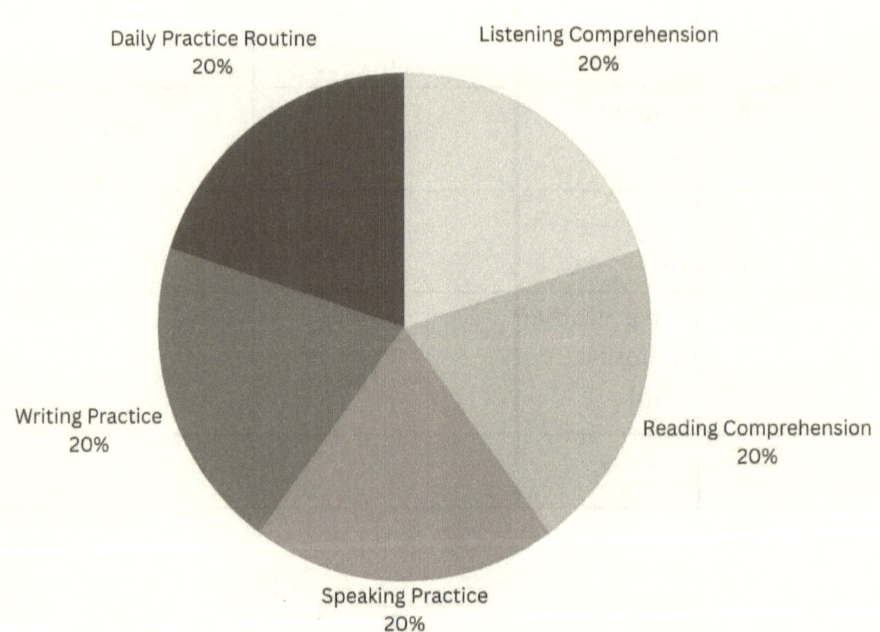

5. TEST STRATEGIES AND PREPARATION

In this section, we'll practise listening comprehension with the following questions. Listen to the provided dialogue and select the appropriate response from the options given.

Listening Section

Type 1 Question and Answer

※[1~4] 다음을 듣고<보기>와같이물음에맞는대답을고르십시오.

<보기>

가: 공책이에요?

나:

❶ 네, 공책이에요.   2 네, 공책이없어요.

3 아니요, 공책이싸요.   4 아니요, 공책이커요.

. (4 점): In this question, we listen to the question being asked and identify the grammar pattern used in the audio. Consequently, the answer should be structured using the same grammar pattern.

1 네, 사람이에요.   2 네, 사람이많아요.

3 아니요, 사람이좋아요.   4 아니요, 사람이있어요.

2. (4 점)

1 네, 노래가있어요.   2 네, 노래를알아요.

3 아니요, 노래를못해요.   4 아니요, 노래가아니에요.

3. (3 점)

1 목요일에봐요.   2 친구를만나요.

3 학교에서봐요.   4 두시에만나요.

Now Try to solve these Questions

Here is the Listening Text for more understanding.

1. (4 점)

여자: 사람이많아요?

남자:

2. (4 점)

남자: 노래를잘해요?

여자:

3. (3 점)

남자: 오늘몇시에만나요?

여자:

Talking about time ,when we meet

Type 2 Greetings

[1] 다음을듣고<보기>와같이이어지는말을고르십시오.

<보기>

가: 안녕히계세요.

나:

1 들어오세요.   2 어서오세요.

3 안녕히계세요.   ❹ 안녕히가세요.

1. (4 점)

1 고맙습니다.   2 괜찮습니다.

3 축하합니다.   4 그렇습니다.

Listening to Text for more understanding

1. (4 점)

여자: 휴가잘다녀오세요.

This means "Have a good vacation." How would you respond to this? "Thank you, ight?"

남자:

Type 3 Choose According to the NOUN

[1] 여기는어디입니까? <보기>와같이알맞은것을고르십시오.

<보기>

가: 내일까지숙제를꼭내세요.

나: 네,선생님·

1 빵집   2 호텔   ❸교실   4 병원

1. (3 점)

1 극장   2 서점   3 약국   4 시장

Listening Text of the above question:

남자: 빨리오세요. 영화가곧시작해요. MOVIE

여자: 네, 지금가요.

Type 4 Choose according to Noun

[1] 다음은무엇에대해말하고있습니까?<보기>와같이알맞은 것을고르십시오

Example

가: 이아파트에살아요?

나: 네, 5 층에살아요.

❶집   2 역   3 주소   4 달력

1. (3 점)

1 이   2 가족   3 직업   4 생일

Listening Text of above question

남자: 안녕하세요? 김준호입니다.

여자: 반갑습니다. 저는이지영입니다.

Here, they are Using Names As Hint

Type 5 Choose the Image According to Audio

[1] 다음 대화를 듣고 알맞은 그림을 고르십시오. (각 4 점)

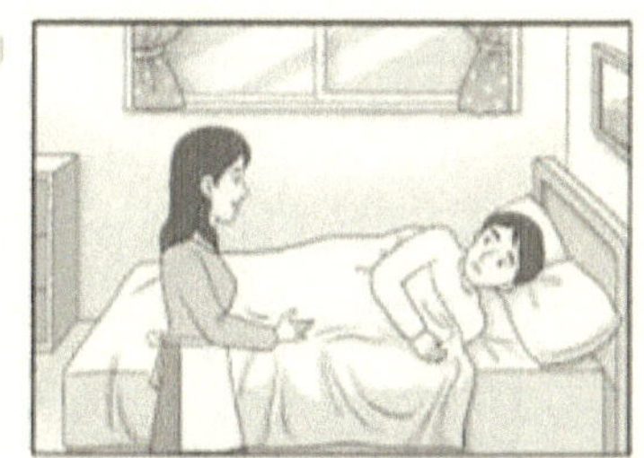

15. Listening text of above question

여자: 일어나서식사하세요.

남자 : 너무 피곤해요. 조금만 더 잘게요.

Type 6 Listen and Choose most Appropriate Statement

[17~21] 다음을듣고<보기>와같이대화내용과같은것을고르십시오. (각 3 점)

<보기>

남자: 요즘한국어를공부해요?

여자: 네. 한국친구한테서한국어를배워요.

1. 1 남자는학생입니다.　　　　2 여자는학교에다닙니다.

2. 3 남자는한국어를가르칩니다.　❹ 여자는한국어를공부합니다.

17.

1. 여자의집은지하철역에서멉니다.

2. 여자는더넓은집으로이사했습니다.

3. 남자는여자의짐이많아서힘들었습니다.

4. 남자는비가와서이사를도와주지못했습니다.

Listening Text of the above Question

17.

여자: 이사도와줘서고마워요. 비도오는데많이힘들었죠?

남자: 뭘요. 짐이많지않아서괜찮았어요. (잠시쉬고) 집이좋네요.

여자: 네. 지난번집보다넓어서좋아요. 지하철역도바로앞에있고요.

Type 7 Choose the answer that corresponds to the question beingasked.

[22~24] 다음을듣고여자의중심생각을고르십시오. (각 3 점)

22.

1. 동네에서자전거를타면안됩니다.

2. 많은사람들이자전거를타야합니다.

3. 안전한자전거도로가생겨서좋습니다.

4. 자전거도로에서도사고가날수있습니다.

Listening text of the above question

22.

남자: 저기좀보세요. 우리동네에도자전거도로가생겼어요.

여자: 그렇네요. 도로에서자전거를탈때마다위험했는데잘됐네요.

남자: 그런데신문에서보니까자전거도로에서도사고가많이나는것 같아요.

여자: 그래요그렇지만자전거도로가생겨서더안전하게탈수있을   것같은데요.

Type 8 Choose the answer that corresponds to the question being asked.

[25~26] 다음을듣고물음에답하십시오.

25.

여자가왜이이야기를하고있는지맞는것을고르십시오. (3 점)

1.   1 회사의특별한날을정하려고

2.   회사의쉬는날을말해주려고

3.   회사의행사준비장소를바꾸려고

4.   회사에서주는선물을알려주려고

26.

들은내용과같은것을고르십시오. (4 점)

1.   1 이회사의식당은 4 층에있습니다.

2.   이회사는수요일마다케이크를줍니다.

3.   가족사랑의날'에는 4 시에퇴근합니다.

4.   가족사랑의날'에는가족들이회사에옵니다.

Listening Text of above question

여자: (딩동댕) 안녕하십니까? 매주수요일은우리회사'가족사랑의날' 입니다. 내일 '가족사랑의날'에는모두 4 시에퇴근하시기바랍니다. 특별히이번에는회사에서케이크를준비했습니다.내일퇴근하실때 3 층에있는식당에서받아가시기바랍니다. 가족들과즐거운시간 보내십시오. 감사합니다. (딩동댕)

Type 9 Conversation Between Two Persons

[27~28] 다음을듣고물음에답하십시오.

27.

두사람이무엇에대해이야기를하고있는지맞는것을고르십시오. (3 점)

1. 1 선물을 사는 장소

2. 선물을 교환하는 방법

3. 선물을 주고 싶은 사람

4. 선물을 교환할 수 있는 기간

28.

들은 내용과 같은 것을 고르십시오. (4 점)

1. 여자는 백화점에 교환권을 사러 갈 겁니다.

2. 여자는 선물 교환을 친구에게 부탁했습니다.

3. 여자는 사이즈가 큰 티셔츠를 선물받았습니다.

4. 여자는 친구에게 주려고 티셔츠를 가지고 왔습니다.

Listening text of question

남자: 어, 이게 뭐예요? 티셔츠네요.

여자: 네. 친구가 선물로 준 건데 사이즈가 좀 커요. 바꾸고 싶은데 선물 받은 거라서 고민이에요.

남자: 혹시 상자 안에 교환권 없어요? 요즘엔 다른 물건으로 바꿀 수 있는 교환권을 선물에 넣어주는데요.

여자: 아, 여기 상자 안에 있네요. 이걸 가지고 가면 바꿀 수 있어요?

남자: 네. 가까운 백화점에 선물 받은 물건과 교환권을 가지고 가면 바꿀 수 있어요.

여자: 친구에게 부탁하지 않고 직접 바꿀 수 있으니까 편하겠네요

Type 10 Choose what explains the Author's intention

[29~30] 다음을 듣고 물음에 답하십시오.

29.

여자는 왜 남자를 찾아왔는지 맞는 것을 고르십시오. (3 점)

1. 만화책을 읽고 싶어서

2. 아이가 공부를 잘 못해서

3. 아이가 책 읽기를 싫어해서

4. 만화책의 좋은 점을 알고 싶어서

30.

들은 내용과 같은 것을 고르십시오. (4 점)

1. 1 요즘 아이들은 만화책을 읽지 않습니다.

2. 만화책으로는 어려운 내용을 이해하기 힘듭니다.

3. 책 내용이 재미있으면 만화책을 찾아서 읽습니다.

4. 만화책을 읽으면 책 읽는 습관을 기를 수 있습니다.

Listening Text of above question

여자: 선생님, 안녕하세요? 요즘 저희 아이가 책을 잘 안 읽어요.

그래서 걱정이 돼서 왔어요.

남자: 네. 여기 앉으세요. (잠시 쉬고) 음   아이가 책 읽는 걸 싫어하면

만화책부터 보여주는 건 어떨까요?

여자: 만화책요? 그러면아이가만화책만좋아하지않을까요?

남자: 아니에요. 만화책이책을읽는데도움이돼요. 만화책에서본내용이

재미있으면다른책도찾아서읽게되니까요.

여자: 아, 그러면책읽는습관을기를수있어서좋을것같네요.

남자: 네.또어려운내용을쉽게이해할수있어서공부에도움도돼요.

그래서요즘아이들은만화책을많이읽어요.

The trick to solve Types

TOPIK 1 questions 1 to 30, which focus on choosing the Keyword. □ Studying word sets related to basic vocabulary terms and closely related verbs, adjectives etc, can enhance your ability to choose the correct answer. (For listening practice daily)

Reading Section

Type 1 Choose the correct word According to topic

[31~33] 무엇에대한이야기입니까? <보기>와같이알맞은것을고르 십시오. (각 2 점)

<보기>

아버지는의사입니다. 어머니는은행원입니다.

1   주말   ❷ 부모   3 병원   4 오빠

1.

선생님은한국사람입니다. 저는프랑스사람입니다.

1 가족   2 나라   3 생일   4 친구

In this question, the discussion pertains to Korea and France. This implies that the conversation revolves around distinct nations. Therefore, the term "나라" means "Country." Is the correct Answer?

<u>The trick to solve Type 1</u>

<u>TOPIK 1 questions 31 to 33, which focus on choosing the topic. □ Studying word sets related to umbrella terms and closely related words can enhance your ability to choose the correct topic.</u>

Type 2 Choose correct Nouns. Adverbs, Adjectives, Preposition

[34~39] <보기>와같이( )에들어갈가장알맞은것을고르 십시오.

<보기>

저는( )에 갔습니다. 책을 샀습니다.

1 극장   ❷ 서점   3 공원   4 세탁소

34. (2 점)

이 사람은 회사원입니다. 학생( ) 아닙니다.

1 이   2 의   3 을   4 과

In this question, the subject particles in the statement "this person is a company worker, not a student" are being discussed. Here, "학생(이)" is the correct particle for this context.

<u>The trick to solve Type 2</u>

<u>TOPIK 1 questions 34 to 39 focus on Postposition. □ Studying location particles</u>

Type 3 Choose the most appropriate Statement

[40~42] 다음을 읽고 맞지 않는 것을 고르십시오. (각 3 점)

40.

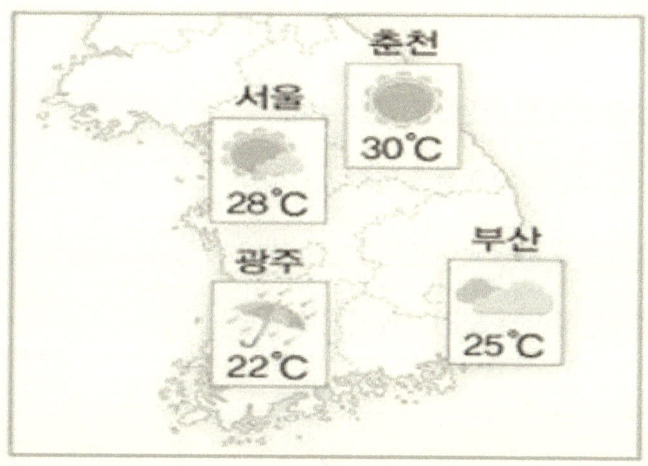

1. 광주는비가옵니다.

2. **서울이 제일 덥습니다**. In this context, we are tasked with identifying the incorrect statement. The image depicts Seoul as being cloudy, which contradicts the claim that Seoul is the hottest. Therefore, the statement "Seoul is the hottest" is incorrect.

3. 부산은날씨가흐립니다.

4. 춘천은날씨가맑습니다.

41.

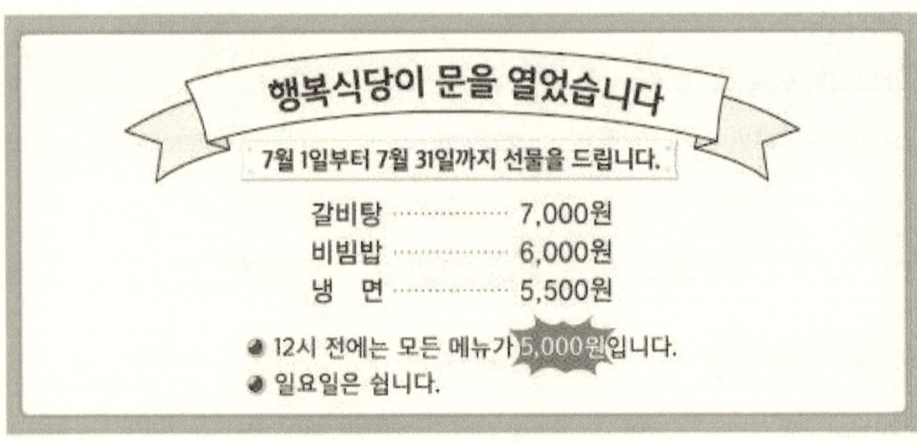

1. 한달동안선물을받을수있습니다.

2. 일요일에는식당이문을열지않습니다.

3. 오후에는갈비탕과비빔밥의값이같습니다.

4. 오전에는냉면을오천원에먹을수있습니다.

42.

시간	8월 7일(금)	
19시	드라마 '우리 집 사람들'	
20시	KBC 뉴스	
21시	영화 '여름 기차'	

1. 영화는뉴스전에합니다.

2. 드라마는한시간정도합니다.

3. 뉴스는저녁여덟시에시작합니다.

4. 팔월칠일밤에영화를볼수있습니다.

To solve this question, we must analyze the information provided in the image. Subsequently, we should identify the statement that aligns with all the given details.

The trick to solve Type 3

TOPIK 1 questions 40 to 42, which focus on the more suitable statement shown in the image. □ Studying these image questions, first, check that all four statements are correct or not then choose the most correct statement that satisfies the image

Type 4 Choose most accurate Statement

[43~45] 다음의내용과같은것을고르십시오.

43. (3 점)

저는한국사람이지만영국에서살고있습니다.

그래서한국어와영어를 모두잘합니다.

지금은일본어를배우고있습니다.

1. 저는일본어를공부합니다.

2. 저는한국어를잘못합니다.

3. 저는지금한국에있습니다.

4. 저는영어를배우고싶습니다.

<u>The trick to solve Type 4</u>

<u>TOPIK 1 questions 43 to 45 focus on the more suitable statement. □ Studying these questions, first, check that all four statements are correct or not then choose the most correct statement that satisfies the above information</u>

Type 5 Choose the correct Statement

[46~48] 다음을읽고중심생각을고르십시오.

46. (3 점)

우리언니는시골학교에서학생들을가르칩니다.

이번주말에언니가 집에올겁니다. 빨리주말이오면좋겠습니다.

1. 저는시골에서살고싶습니다.

2. 저는언니를빨리보고싶습니다.

3. 저는주말에집에가고싶습니다.

4. 저는언니학교에서공부하고싶습니다.

<u>The trick to solve Type 5</u>

<u>TOPIK 1 questions 46 to 48, which focus on the Main text. □ Studying these questions, first we need to choose the keyword for the correct answer.</u>

Type 6 Choose correct Word and Main Idea

[49~50] 다음을읽고물음에답하십시오. (각 2 점)

우리회사지하에는운동하는방,　책을읽는방,　낮잠을자는방,　이야기하는 방이있습니다.　　이방들은점심시간에만문을엽니다.　　우리회사사람들은 이곳을좋아합니다. 이방에가고싶은사람들은(　　가　　) 바로지하로　갑니다. 식사후에짧은시간동안하고싶은것을할수있기때문입니다.

49.

ᄀ에 들어갈 알맞은 말을 고르십시오.

1 책을읽고　　　　　　　　　　　　2 잠을자고

3 일을하고　　　　　　　　　　　　4 밥을먹고

50.

이글의내용과같은것을고르십시오.

1.　1 우리회사식당은지하에있습니다.

2.　우리회사에서는낮잠을잘수없습니다.

3.　우리회사지하에있는방은인기가많습니다.

4.　우리회사사람들은저녁에지하에서운동합니다.

<u>**The trick to solve Type 6**</u>

<u>**TOPIK 1 questions 49 to 50, which focus on the Vocabulary. □ Studying 49 questions, first we need to Read the options and find it is adjectives (conjunctive Adverbs, Phrases) and for question 50 choose the correct statement.**</u>

Type 7 Choose the Correct Grammar and Main Idea of the Article

[51~52] 다음을 읽고 물음에 답하십시오.

눈은 한 번 나빠지면 다시 좋아지기 힘듭니다. 그래서 눈이 나빠지기 전에 눈 건강을 지켜야 합니다.   눈에 좋은 음식을 (________ 가 ________) 눈 운동을 하면 눈 건강에 좋습니다. 그리고 멀리 있는 산이나 나무를 보는 것도 좋습니다. 하지만 눈이 피곤할 때는 눈을 감고 쉬는 것이 제일 좋습니다.

51.

㉠에 들어갈 알맞은 말을 고르십시오. (3 점)

1 먹지만   2 먹거나

3 먹는데   4 먹으면

52.

무엇에 대한 이야기인지 맞는 것을 고르십시오. (2 점)

1 눈에 좋은 음식   2 눈이 나빠지는 이유

3 눈 운동을 하는 시간   4 눈 건강을 지키는 방법

The trick to solve Type 7

TOPIK 1 questions 51 to 52, which focus on the correct Topic. □ Studying these questions, first we need to choose the keyword for the correct answer.

Type 8 Choose the correct Statement and Which Statement Matches the Article's Idea

[53~54] 다음을 읽고 물음에 답하십시오.

저는목소리가아주큽니다.작게말하려고하지만제목소리는다른
사람보다큽니다그래서많은사람들이제목소리를싫어합니다.
그러나우리할머니는제목소리를아주좋아하십니다. 할머니가(____ 가 ____) 때
문입니다. 그래서저는시간이날때마다할머니댁에가서책과신문을읽어드립니다.

53.

ㄱ에 들어갈 알맞은 말을 고르십시오. (2 점)

1 말씀을잘안하시기   2 듣는것을좋아하시기

3 말씀하는것을좋아하시기   4 작은소리를잘못들으시기

54.이글의내용과같은것을고르십시오. (3 점)

1. 1 저는할머니와같이살고있습니다.

2. 제목소리를좋아하는사람들이많습니다.

3. 우리할머니는큰목소리를좋아하십니다.

4. 사람들은보통제목소리를잘못듣습니다.

<u>The trick to solve Type 8</u>

<u>TOPIK 1 questions 53 to 54, which focus on the Main text.</u> 📝 **<u>Studying these questions, first we need to choose the keyword for the correct answer.</u>**

Type 9 Choose the correct connector and Main idea

[55~56] 다음을읽고물음에답하십시오.

우리동네에는'웃음극장'이있습니다.저는힘들때마다이극장에갑니다.
이곳에가면재미있는공연을볼수있기때문입니다.그런데이극장은들어
갈때돈을내지않고나갈때돈을냅니다.이극장에는카메라들이있어서

사람들의웃는모습을찍습니다.크게많이웃으면돈을적게내고적게웃으면돈을많이냅니다. (___가___)사람들은이곳에서많이웃으려고합니다.

55.

ㄱ에 들어갈 알맞은 말을 고르십시오. (2 점)

1 그러면   2 그리고

3 그러나   4 그래서

56.이글의내용과같은것을고르십시오. (3 점)

1. 1 저는웃음극장에서공연을준비합니다.

2. 저는기분이좋으면웃음극장에갑니다.

3. 웃음극장에서는사람들의사진을찍습니다.

4. 웃음극장에서는사람들에게돈을받지않습니다.

<u>The trick to solve Type 9</u>

<u>TOPIK 1 questions 55 to 56, which focus on the Main text. ☐ Studying these questions, first we need to choose the keyword for the correct answer</u>.

Type 10 Arranging Statements correctly

[57~58] 다음을순서대로맞게나열한것을고르십시오.

57. (3 점)

(가) 볼펜으로글을쓰면지우개로지울수없습니다.

(나) 내일쓰기시험을볼때이볼펜을사용하려고합니다.

(다)그런데지우개로지울수있는볼펜을친구한테서받았습니다.

(라) 그러면잘못쓴글을쉽게지울수가있어서편할것같습니다.

<u>**The sentences that begin with "so" are not considered starting statements.**</u>

1 (가)-(나)-(다)-(라)   2 (가)-(나)-(라)-(다)

3 (가)-(다)-(나)-(라)   4 (가)-(다)-(라)-(나)

<u>The trick to solve Type 10</u>

<u>**TOPIK 1 questions 57 to 58, which focus on Arranging the statements.** 📝 **Studying these questions, first we need to check Option, choose the keyword for the correct answer, and then check the correct order: if there is a pronoun in a statement then it will not be a first statement.**</u>

Type 11 Correct Statement and Main Idea

[59~60] 다음을읽고물음에답하십시오.

걷기는많은사람들이쉽게할수있는운동입니다(가)것은건강에도움이많이됩니다.(가)것이아니고온몸이움직이게되기때문입니다.(가)그런데걷기운동을할때에는천천히걷기시작해서조금씩빨리걷는것이좋습니다.(ㄹ) 이렇게 하는 것이 건강에 도움이 더 많이 됩니다.

59.다음문장이들어갈곳을고르십시오. (2 점)

어린아이부터나이가많은사람까지모두쉽게할수있습니다.

1. ㄱ   2 ㄴ   3 ㄷ   4 ㄹ

60.이글의내용과같은것을고르십시오. (3 점)

1. 1 사람들은걸을때온몸이움직이게됩니다.

2. 다리만움직이면서걷는것이건강에좋습니다.

3. 걷기운동은처음부터빨리걷는것이좋습니다.

4. 천천히오래걷는것이건강에더도움이됩니다.

<u>The trick to solve Type 11</u>

<u>TOPIK 1 questions 59 to 60, which focus on the Main text. ☐ Studying these questions, first we need to choose the appropriate statement position for the correct answer.</u>

Type 12 Correct word and the Main idea of the Paragraph

[61~62] 다음을 읽고 물음에 답하십시오. (각 2 점)

제 이름은 김둘입니다. 바라셨습니다. 그래서 숫자 2 로 이름을 지어주셨습니다. 덕분에 사람들이 저를 잘 기억합니다. 그리고 다른 사람들과 쉽게 친구가 될 수 있습니다. 할아버지께서 지어주신 이름의 의미처럼 제 옆에는 항상 친구가 있습니다. 그래서 (_____ 가 _____) 행복합니다.

61.

ㄱ에 들어갈 알맞은 말을 고르십시오.

1 아프지 않고

2 외롭지 않고

3 바쁘지 않고

4 급하지 않고

62.

이 글의 내용과 같은 것을 고르십시오.

1. 우리 할아버지의 이름은 김둘입니다.

2. 사람들은 제 이름을 잘 잊어버립니다.

3. 제 이름에는 특별한 의미가 있습니다.

4. 저는 이름 때문에 친구를 사귀기 힘듭니다.

<u>The trick to solve Type 12</u>

<u>TOPIK 1 questions 61 to 62, which focus on the Main text. ☐ Studying question 61, first we need to choose the correct word and for question 62 we choose the correct Statement.</u>

Type 13 E-mail, Notifications, Article

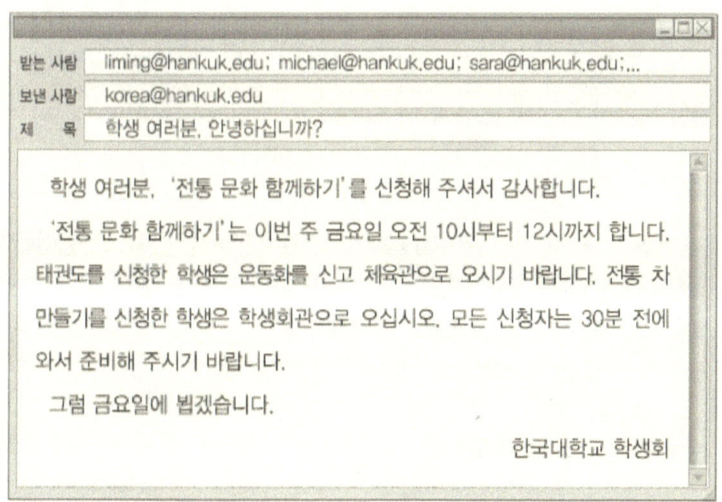

63.

학생회에서는왜이글을썼는지맞는것을고르십시오. (2 점)

1. 1 전통문화함께하기를소개하려고

2. 전통문화함께하기신청자를확인하려고

3. 전통문화함께하기신청방법을알려주려고

4. 전통문화함께하기시간과장소를안내하려고

64.

이글의내용과같은것을고르십시오. (3 점)

1.   1 신청자는모두운동화를신어야합니다.

2.   신청자는아홉시반까지모여야합니다.

3.   신청자는금요일까지전통차를준비해야합니다.

4.   신청자는체육관에모인후에학생회관으로갈겁니다.

<u>The trick to solve Type 13</u>

<u>TOPIK 1 questions 63 to 64, which focus on the Main text. ☐ Studying question 63, first we need to check the author's intention for the correct answer and the question 65, we choose the correct statement.</u>

Type14 Comprehension

[65~66] 다음을읽고물음에답하십시오.

저는(________ 가 ________)오랫동안생각만하고빨리결정하지못합니다.결정하는 것이어려워서혼자서는필요한물건을잘고르지못합니다.그래서저는 친구가옆에있으면친구가하는것을따라합니다.그렇게하면제가 결정하지않아도돼서마음이편합니다.하지만지금부터는제가작은 일부터하나씩결정해보려고합니다.

65.

그에 들어갈 알맞은 말을 고르십시오. (2 점)

1 마음이편할때   2 힘든일을할때

3 친구가생각날때   4 어떤것을선택할때

66.

이글의내용과같은것을고르십시오. (3 점)

1. 1 제친구는내결정을따라합니다.

2. 저는오래생각하지않고결정합니다.

3. 저는앞으로친구와함께결정할겁니다.

4. 저는혼자물건을고르는것이어렵습니다.

The trick to solve Type 14

TOPIK 1 questions 65 to 66, which focus on the Main text. ☐ Studying question 65, first we need to choose the right word for the correct answer and the question 66, we choose the correct statement.

Type 15 Comprehension

[67~68] 다음을읽고물음에답하십시오. (각 3 점)

사람들은결혼할때보통많은사람들을초대합니다.다른사람들에게 결혼하는모습을보여주고싶기때문입니다.가까운친구들만(________ 가 ________) 작은결혼식'을하는사람들이생겼습니다.이런결혼식을하는사람들은적은돈으 로결혼을준비합니다. 이렇게 하면서가까운사람들과함께결혼의기쁨을나눕니다.

67.

㉠에 들어갈 알맞은 말을 고르십시오.

1 초대해서   2 초대해도

3 초대하거나   4 초대하려면

68.

이글의내용과같은것을고르십시오.

1. 1 이결혼식은돈이많이들지않습니다.

2. 이결혼식을하는사람이많아졌습니다.

3. 이결혼식에사람들을많이초대합니다.

4. 이결혼식은보여주는것이중요합니다.

The trick to solve Type 15

TOPIK 1 questions 67 to 68, which focus on the Main text. ☐ Studying question 67, first we need to choose the right word with grammar for the correct answer and the question 68, we choose the correct statement.

Type 16 Comprehension

[69~70] 다음을읽고물음에답하십시오. (각 3 점)

아버지는요리에관심이없어서거의요리를하지않으셨습니다.그런데 지난달에어머니가다리를다쳐서요리를못하게되었습니다.그때부터 아버지는요리를(　　가　　).아버지의요리는맛있을때도있고맛없을때도있었습 니다.드셨습니다. 그후로아버지는요리하는것을좋아하게되셨습니다.

69.

ㄱ에 들어갈 알맞은 말을 고르십시오.

1 하실수없었습니다　　　　　　　　　　2 하실것같았습니다

3 하시기시작했습니다　　　　　　　　　4 해주신적이없었습니다

70.

이글의내용으로알수있는것을고르십시오.

1. 1 아버지는요즘요리에관심을갖게되셨습니다.

2. 아버지는오래전부터요리학원에다니셨습니다.

3. 어머니는아버지가요리하는것을도와주셨습니다.

4. 아버지가만든음식의맛이점점좋아지고있습니다.

<u>The trick to solve Type 16</u>

<u>TOPIK 1 questions 69 to 70, which focus on the Main text.</u> **<u>Studying question 69, first we need to choose the right tense with a word for the correct answer and the question 70, we choose the correct statement.</u>**

CONCLUSION

Well done! You've made it to the end of "Mastering TOPIK 1: Your Ultimate Guide to Success in15 Days." What a journey it's been! From getting to grips with the ins and outs of the TOPIK 1 exam to mastering those tricky grammar rules and expanding your vocabulary, you've put in the effort over the past two weeks.

Now, as you take a moment to look back on how far you've come, remember that learning a language is all about the journey, not just the destination. While this guide has given you the toolsand strategies you need to tackle the TOPIK 1 exam, it's only the beginning of your language- learning adventure.

As you gear up for exam day, take a deep breath and trust in yourself. You've put in the work, andyou're more than ready to show what you can do.

Whether you're aiming to open up new career opportunities, connect more deeply with Korean culture, or simply challenge yourself, passing the TOPIK 1 exam is a huge achievement.

And remember, this isn't the end of your language learning journey – it's just a milestone along theway. Keep exploring, keep practising, and keep pushing yourself to new heights.

TRANSLATED VERSION

Listening Section

Type 1 Question and Answer

*[1-4] Listen to the following and select the answer that fits the question, such as <View>.

<View

A: Is that a notebook?

I:

① Yes, it's a notebook.　　　2 Yes, I don't have a notebook.

3 No, notebooks are cheap.　　　4 No, it's a notebook wicker.

1. (4 points): In this question, we listen to the question being asked and identify the grammar pattern used in the audio. Consequently, the answer should be structured using the same grammar pattern.

1 Yes, it's a person.　　　2 Yes, there are a lot of people.

3 No, I like people.　　　4 No, I have a person.

2. (4 points)

1 Yes, I have the song.　　　2 Yes, I know the song.

3 No, I don't sing.　　　4 No, I don't sing.

3. (3 points)

1 See you on Thursday.　　　2 Meet a friend.

3 See you at school.　　　4 See you at two.

Now Try to solve these Questions

Here is the Listening Text for more understanding.

1. (4 points)

Woman: Is it crowded?

Man:

2. (4 points)

Man: Are you a good singer?

Woman:

3. (3 points)

Man: What time are we meeting today?

Woman:

Talking about time, when we meet

Type 2 Greetings

[5-6] Listen to the following and select the words that follow, such as <View>.

<View>

Go: Goodbye.

I:

1 Come in.   2 Welcome.

3 Goodbye.   ❹Goodbye.

1. (4 points)

1 Thank you.   2 No problem.

3 Congratulations.   4 That's right.

Listening to Text for more understanding

1. (4 points)

Woman: Have a great vacation.

Man:

This means "Have a good vacation." How would you respond to this? "Thank you, right?"

Type 3 Choose According to the NOUN

[7-10] Select the appropriate one, such as Where am I?

<View>

A: Get your homework done by tomorrow.

Me: Yes, sir.   .

1 Bakeries   2 Hotels   ❸Classroom   4 Hospitals

1. (3 points)

1 Theater   2 Bookstores   3 Pharmacy   4 Markets

Listening Text of the above question:

man: Hurry up. The movie's about to start. MOVIE

Woman: Yes, I'm on my way.

Type 4 Choose according to Noun

[11-14] What is the following talking about, such as <View>, and pick the right one.

Example

A: Do you live in this apartment?

Me: Yes, I live on the fifth floor.

❶ Home   2 Stations   3 Addresses   4 Calendar

2. (3 points)

1 This 2 Family   3 Occupation   4 Birthdays

Listening Text of above question

Man: How are you? This is Junho Kim.

Woman: Nice to meet you, my name is Jiyoung Lee.

Here, they are Using Names As Hin t

Type 5 Choose the Image According to Audio

[15-16]   Next   Conversation   listen to   the right   picture the correct picture. (Each   4 points)

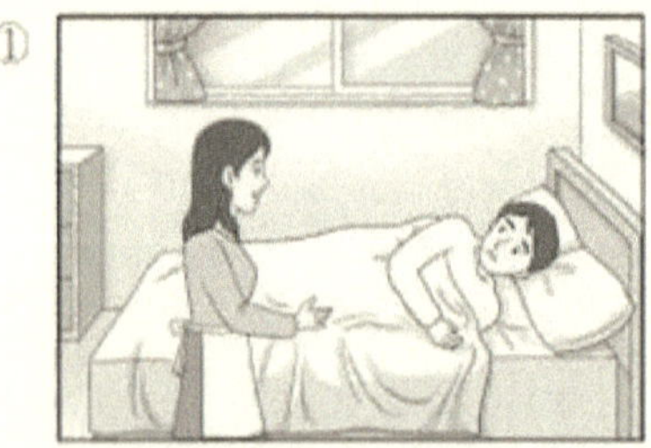

15. Listening text of above question

   Woman: Get up and eat.

   Man: I'm very tired, I'll sleep a little longer.

Type 6 Listen and Choose most Appropriate Statement

[17-21] Listen to the following and select a transcript of the conversation, such as <show>. (3 points each)

<View

Man: Are you studying Korean these days?

Woman: Yes. I learn Korean from my Korean friend.

1   The man is a student.   2 The woman goes to school.

3 A man teaches Korean.   ❹ Women study Korean.

17.

5.   The woman's house is far from the subway station.

6.   The woman moved to a larger house.

7.   Men have a hard time with women's burdens.

8.   The man could not help but move because of the rain.

Listening Text of the above Question

17.

Woman: Thank you for the isadō. It's raining a lot, isn't it?

Man: Well, I didn't have much luggage, so it was fine. (Pause) Nice house.

Woman: Yes. It's bigger than my last place, so it's nice, and the subway station is right in front.

Type 7 Choose the answer that corresponds to the question being asked.

[22-24] Identify the woman's central idea based on the following: (3 points each)

22.

> 5. You shouldn't ride a bike in your neighborhood.
>
> 6. Many people need to ride a bike.
>
> 7. It's nice to have safe bike lanes.
>
> 8. Accidents can also happen on bike paths.

Listening text of the above question

22.

man: Look at that. My neighborhood just got a bike lane.

Woman: That's good, because every time I ride my bike on the road, it's dangerous.

Man: But I read in the newspaper that there are a lot of accidents on bike paths.

Woman: Yes, but I think the bike lanes will make it safer.

Type 8 Choose the answer that corresponds to the question being asked.

[25-26] Listen to the following and answer the questions.

25.

Choose the correct explanation for why the woman is telling this story. (3 points)

> 1   1 You want to organize a special day for your company
>
> 2   to tell me the company's holiday
>
> 3   To change your company's event staging location
>
> 4   To announce a gift from your company

26.

Choose something like what you heard. (4 points)

> 1   1 The company's cafeteria is on the fourth floor.

2   This company gives out cakes every Wednesday.

3   On Family Love Day, I leave work at 4:00.

4   On Family Love Day, families come to work.

Listening Text of above question

Woman: (Ding dong dong) Good morning, every Wednesday is our company's Family Love Day.   Tomorrow is Family Love Day, and we ask everyone to leave work at 4:00. Specially this time, the company has prepared a cake for you, please pick it up at the cafeteria on the third floor when you leave work tomorrow. Have a good time with your families. Thank you. (ding dong ding)

Type 9 Conversation Between Two Persons

[27-28] Listen to the following and answer the questions.

27.

Choose the correct statement about what the two people are talking about. (3 points)

1   1 Where to buy gifts

2   How to exchange gifts

3   To whom you want to give a gift

4   How long you can exchange gifts

28.

Choose something like what you heard. (4 points)

1   She's going to the department store to buy a voucher.

2   The woman asked her friend to exchange gifts.

3   A woman is gifted an oversized T-shirt.

4   The woman brought a T-shirt to give to her friend.

Listening text of question

Man: Uh, what is this? It's a T-shirt.

Woman: Yes. It was a gift from a friend, but it's a little big, and I'd like to change it, but it was a gift.

Man: Isn't there a voucher in the box? These days, they put a voucher in the gift that can be redeemed for something else.

Woman: Oh, it's in a box here, can I take this and change it?

Man: Yes. You can take your gift to the nearest department store and get a voucher to exchange it.

Woman: It must be nice to be able to change it yourself without having to ask a friend.

Type 10 Choose what explains the Author's intention

[29-30] Listen to the following and answer the questions.

29.

Choose the correct answer to why the woman came looking for the man. (3 points)

1　I want to read a comic book

2　The child is not studying well

3　My child doesn't like to read.

4　I want to know what's good about comic books

30.

Choose something like what you heard. (4 points)

5.　1 Kids don't read comic books these days.

6.　It's hard to understand what's going on in a comic book.

7.　If the book is interesting, I find a comic book and read it.

8.   Reading comic books can help you get into the habit of reading.

Listening Text of above question

Woman: Teacher, how are you? My child hasn't been reading much lately.

So I came here because I was worried.

man: Yeah. Have a seat. (Pause) Um. If your child doesn't like to read, you can try

Why not start with comic books?

Woman: Comic books? Doesn't that mean he only likes comic books?

Man: No. Comic books help me read books, because what I see in the comic books is what I've seen in

Because if it's interesting, you'll find other books to read.

Woman: Oh, that would be great to get me in the habit of reading.

Man: Yes. It also helps me study because it makes difficult content easy to understand.

So kids read a lot of comic books these days.

<u>The trick to solve Types</u>

<u>TOPIK 1 questions 1 to 30, which focus on choosing the Keyword. □ Studying word sets related to basic vocabulary terms and closely related verbs, adjectives etc, can enhance your ability to choose the correct answer. (For listening practice daily)</u>

Reading Section

Type 1 Choose the correct word According to topic

[31-33] What is the story about? Choose the correct one, such as <example>. (2 points each)

<View>?

My father is a doctor. My mother is a banker.

1.Weekend   ❷ Parents   3 Hospital   4 Brother

31.

You are Korean. I am French.

1 Families   2 Country   3 Birthdays   4 Friends

In this question, the discussion pertains to Korea and France. This implies that the conversation revolves around distinct nations. Therefore, the term "나라" means "Country." Is the correct Answer?

<u>The trick to solve Type 1</u>

<u>TOPIK 1 questions 31 to 33, which focus on choosing the topic. ☐ Studying word sets related to umbrella terms and closely related words can enhance your ability to choose the correct topic.</u>

Type 2 Choose correct Nouns. Adverbs, Adjectives, Preposition

[34-39] Select the most appropriate one to enter ( ), such as <View>.

<View>

I went to ( ) and bought a book.

1 Theater   ❷ Bookstores 3 Parks   4 Laundromats

34. (2 points)

This person is an employee, not a student ( ).

1 this   2 of   3 を   4 and

In this question, the subject particles in the statement "this person is a company worker, not a student" are being discussed. Here, "student(s)" is the correct particle for this context.

<u>The trick to solve Type 2</u>

<u>TOPIK 1 questions 34 to 39 focus on Postposition. ☐ Studying location particles</u>

Type 3 Choose the most appropriate Statement

[40-42] Read the following and select the one that is not correct. (3 points each)

40.

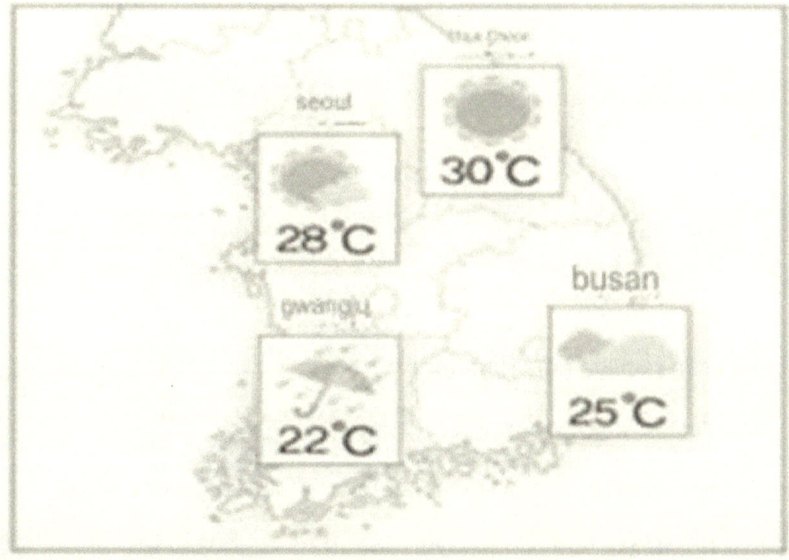

1 It's raining.

2 **<u>Seoul is the</u>** hottest city. In this context, we are tasked with identifying the incorrect statement. The image depicts Seoul as being cloudy, which contradicts the claim that Seoul is the hottest. Therefore, the statement "Seoul is the hottest" is incorrect.

3 It is cloudy in Busan.

4 Chuncheon is a sunny city.

41.

1 You can receive gifts for a month.

2 The restaurant is not open on Sundays.

3 In the afternoon, galbitang and bibimbap are the same price.

4 For breakfast, you can eat cold noodles for 5,000 won.

42.

1   The movie is before the news.

2   The drama lasts about an hour.

3   News starts at 8pm.

4   You can watch a movie on August 7th night.

To solve this question, we must analyze the information provided in the image. Subsequently, we should identify the statement that aligns with all the given details.

The trick to solve Type 3

TOPIK 1 questions 40 to 42, which focus on the more suitable statement shown in the image. ☐ Studying these image questions, first, check that all four statements are correct or not then choose the most correct statement that satisfies the image

Type 4 Choose most accurate Statement

[43-45] Select something like the following

43. (3 points)

I'm Korean, but I live in the UK.

So, I'm good at both Korean and English.

I'm currently learning Japanese.

1   I'm studying Japanese.

2   I don't speak Korean well.

3   I'm in South Korea right now.

4   I want to learn English.

<u>The trick to solve Type 4</u>

<u>TOPIK 1 questions 43 to 45 focus on the more suitable statement. ☐ Studying these questions, first, check that all four statements are correct or not then choose the most correct statement that satisfies the above information</u>

Type 5 Choose the correct Statement

[46-48] Read the following and select a central thought.

46. (3 points)

My sister teaches students in a rural school.

My sister will be home at the end of this week, I can't wait for the weekend.

1   I want to live in the countryside.

2   I can't wait to see my sister.

3   I want to go home for the weekend.

4   I want to study at my sister's school.

<u>The trick to solve Type 5</u>

<u>TOPIK 1 questions 46 to 48, which focus on the Main text. ☐ Studying these questions, first we need to choose the keyword for the correct answer.</u>

Type 6 Choose correct Word and Main Idea

[49-50] Read the following and answer the questions. (2 points each)

In the basement of our company, we have a room to work out, a room to read, a room to nap, and a room to talk. These rooms are only open during lunch. People in our company like this place. People who want to go to this room go (go) straight to the basement. That's because they can do whatever they want for a short time after eating.

49.

Choose the right word for ⌐.

1 Read a book   2 Sleeping

3 Doing work   4 eat rice

50.

Choose something like the one in this article.

1   1 Our cafeteria is in the basement.

2   You can't take a nap in my company.

3   The room in the basement of our company is very popular.

4   My company people exercise underground in the evening.

<u>The trick to solve Type 6</u>

<u>TOPIK 1 questions 49 to 50, which focus on the Vocabulary. □ Studying 49 questions, first we need to Read the options and find it is adjectives (conjunctive Adverbs, Phrases) and for question 50 choose the correct statement.</u>

Type 7 Choose the Correct Grammar and Main Idea of the Article

[51-52] Read the following and answer the questions.

Once your eyes get bad, it's hard to get them good again, so you need to take care of them before they get worse. Eating foods that <u>are</u> good for your eyes, doing eye exercises, and looking at distant mountains and trees are good for your eyes, but when your eyes are tired, it's best to close them and rest.

51.

Choose an appropriate word for ㄱ. (3 points)

1 eat but   2 eat or

3 To eat   4 When you eat

52.

Choose the correct answer to what the story is about. (2 points)

1 Foods for the eyes   2 Reasons for bad eyes

3 How long to do eye exercises   4 How to Protect Your Eye Health

The trick to solve Type 7

TOPIK 1 questions 51 to 52, which focus on the correct Topic. ☐ Studying these questions, first we need to choose the keyword for the correct answer.

Type 8 Choose the correct Statement and Which Statement Matches the Article's Idea

[53-54] Read the following and answer the questions.

I have a loud voice.I try to speak small, but my voice is louder than other people's.So many people don't like my voice.But my grandmother likes my voice very much. That's why I go to my grandmother's house whenever I have time____read her books and newspapers.

53.

Choose an appropriate word for ㄱ. (2 points)

1 Not being a good speaker   2 Love to listen

3 You love to talk   4 You mishear small sounds

54. Choose something like the content of this article. (3 points)

   1   I live with my grandmother.

   2   Many people like the sound of the title.

   3   My grandmother likes loud voices.

   4   People don't listen to supervisory voices.

The trick to solve Type 8

TOPIK 1 questions 53 to 54, which focus on the Main text. Studying these questions, first we need to choose the keyword for the correct answer.

Type 9 Choose the correct connector and Main idea

[55-56] Read the following and answer the questions.

In my neighborhood, there is a "Laughter Theater." I go to this theater whenever I have a hard time. But this theater doesn't pay when you go in, you pay when you leave. There are cameras in this theater to film people laughing.If you laugh a lot, you pay __________, and if you laugh a little, you pay a lot.(a)People try to laugh a lot in this place.

55.

Choose an appropriate word for ㄱ. (2 points)

1 And then   2 and then

3 But   4 So

56. Choose something like the content of this article. (3 points)

   1   1 I am preparing to perform at the Laughing Theater.

   2   I go to the comedy theater when I'm in the mood.

   3   Laughter Theater takes pictures of people.

   4   Laughter theaters don't charge people money.

<u>The trick to solve Type 9</u>

<u>TOPIK 1 questions 55 to 56, which focus on the Main text. ☐ Studying these questions, first we need to choose the keyword for the correct answer</u>.

Type 10 Arranging Statements correctly

[57-58] Select the correct number of the following, in order

57. (3 points)

(a) If you write with a ballpoint pen, you can't erase it with an eraser.

(b) I am going to use this ballpoint pen tomorrow when I take a writing test.

(C) But then I got a ballpoint pen from a friend that can only be erased with an eraser.

(d) It would be nice to be able to easily delete a mistake.

<u>The sentences that begin with "so" are not considered starting statements.</u>

1 (a)-(b)-(c)-(d)-(e)   2 (a)-(b)-(c)-(d)

3 (a)-(c)-(d)-(e)-(f)   4 (a)-(c)-(d)-(e)-(f)

<u>The trick to solve Type 10</u>

<u>TOPIK 1 questions 57 to 58, which focus on Arranging the statements. Studying these questions, first we need to check Option, choose the keyword for the correct answer, and then check the correct order: if there is a pronoun in a statement then it will not be a first statement.</u>

Type 11 Correct Statement and Main Idea

[59-60] Read the following and answer the questions.

Walking is an easy exercise for many people to do(a) and it is very beneficial to your health(b) because it gets your whole body moving.(c) However, when you are doing walking exercises, it is recommended that you start walking slowly and then walk faster in small increments.(=) This way, your health will benefit more.

59. Choose the place where the following sentence would go. (2 points)

It's easy for kids and adults alike.

1. ㄱ 　　　　　2 ㄴ 　　　　　3 ㄷ 　　　　　4 ㄹ

60. Choose something like the content of this article. (3 points)

   1   People move their whole body when they walk.

   2   Walking with only your legs moving is good for your health.

   3   Walking is a good place to start.

   4   Slow, long walks are better for your health.

The trick to solve Type 11

TOPIK 1 questions 59 to 60, which focus on the Main text. □ Studying these questions, first we need to choose the appropriate statement position for the correct answer.

Type 12 Correct word and the Main idea of the Paragraph

[61-62] Read the following and answer the questions. (2 points each)

Jamie is two, as my grandfather wanted, so he named me with the number two. Thanks to this, people remember me well, and I can easily make friends with others. Just like the meaning of my grandfather's name, I always have a friend by my side. That___makes me happy.

61.

Choose the right word for ㄱ.

1 Not sick 　　　　　　　　　　2 Not lonely

3 Not busy 　　　　　　　　　　4 Not in a hurry

62.

Choose something like the one in this article.

1   My grandfather's name is Kim Doo.

2   People forget names.

3   There's something special about a name.

4   I have a hard time making friends because of my name.

<u>The trick to solve Type 12</u>

<u>TOPIK 1 questions 61 to 62, which focus on the Main text. ☐ Studying question 61, first we need to choose the correct word and for question 62 we choose the correct Statement.</u>

Type 13 E-mail, Notifications, Article

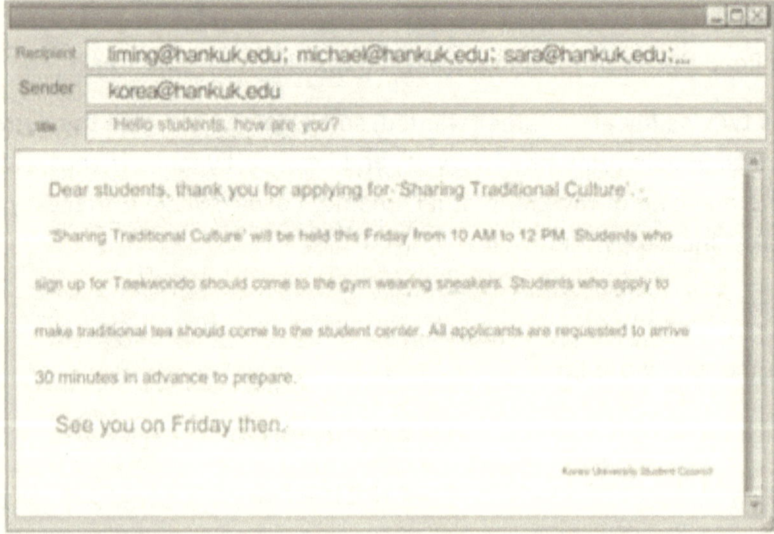

63.

For the correct answer, identify why the student government wrote the letter. (2 points)

    1   To introduce Traditional Culture Together

    2   Join the traditionTo verify an applicant

    3   To let you know how to apply for a traditional culture share

    4   TraditionCultureTogetherTimes and PlacesTo guide you

64.

Choose something like the content of this article (3 points)

    1   1 All applicants must wear sneakers.

    2   Applicants must gather by 9:30am.

    3   Applicants must have a traditional car ready by Friday.

    4   Applicants will gather in the gym and then go to the student center.

<u>The trick to solve Type 13</u>

<u>TOPIK 1 questions 63 to 64, which focus on the Main text. ☐ Studying question 63, first we need to check the author's intention for the correct answer and the question 65, we choose the correct statement</u>.

Type14 Comprehension

[65-66] Read the following and answer the questions.

I( ) think for a long time and don't decide quickly.It's hard for me to decide, so I can't pick out the things I need by myself.So when I have a friend by my side, I follow what he does.That way I don't have to decide and I feel relaxed.But from now on, I'm going to try to decide one small thing at a time.

65.

Choose an appropriate word for ㄱ. (2 points)

1 When it's easy   2 When doing hard work

3 When you think of a friend   4 When choosing something

66.

Choose something like the content of this article (3 points)

1   My friend follows my decision.

2   I don't think long before I make a decision.

3   I'll decide with my friend in the future.

4   I'm afraid to pick things by myself.

The trick to solve Type 14

TOPIK 1 questions 65 to 66, which focus on the Main text. ☐ Studying question 65, first we need to choose the right word for the correct answer and the question 66, we choose the correct statement.

Type 15 Comprehension

[67-68] Read the following and answer the questions. (3 points each)

People usually invite a lot of people when they get married because they want to show other people what it's like to get married. Some people have "small weddings" with only their close friends. This way, they share the joy of marriage with people close to them.

67.

Choose the right word for ㄱ.

1 By invitation   2 Even if you invite

3 To invite or   4 To invite

68.

Choose something like the one in this article.

1   This wedding doesn't cost a lot of money.

2   More people are getting married.

3   I'm inviting a lot of people to this wedding.

4   This wedding is all about show.

The trick to solve Type 15

TOPIK 1 questions 67 to 68, which focus on the Main text. □ Studying question 67, first we need to choose the right word with grammar for the correct answer and the question 68, we choose the correct statement.

Type 16 Comprehension

[69-70] Read the following and answer the questions. (3 points each)

My father rarely cooked because he was not interested in cooking, but last month my mother hurt her leg and couldn't cook anymore.Since then my father <u>has been cooking( )</u>.My father's cooking is sometimes good and sometimes bad. Since then my father has become a big fan of cooking.

69.

Choose the right word for ⌐.

1 Can't do it   2 I thought you would

3 I'm starting to do it   4 Never done it

70.

Choose the one that you can tell from the content of this article.

    1   My father has recently become interested in cooking.

    2   My father has been going to culinary school for a long time.

    3   My mother used to help my father cook.

    4   My father's food is getting better and better.

<u>The trick to solve Type 16</u>

<u>TOPIK 1 questions 69 to 70, which focus on the Main text. Studying question 69, first we need to choose the right tense with a word for the correct answer and the question 70, we choose the correct statement.</u>